Organized Crime Queens
The Secret World of Female Gangsters

By Jerry Bader

From the bizarre world of female Japanese motorcycle gangs to the historic rise and fall of London's Forty Elephants, the history of female organized crime is both fascinating and strange.

These are the stories, both true and legendary of the female crime bosses that broke the mould of feminine gentility. This is *The Secret World of Female Gangsters*.

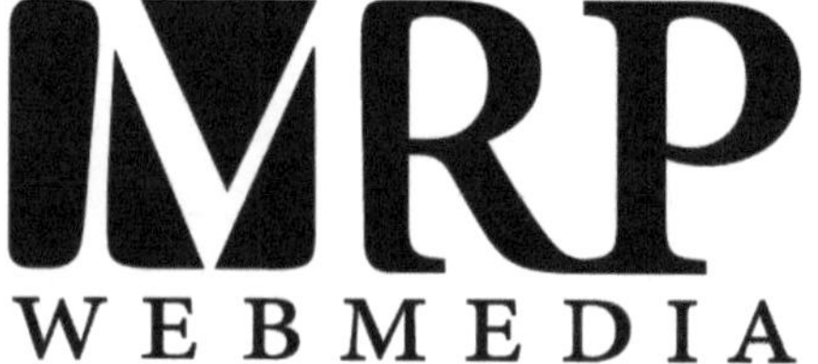

Organized Crime Queens

The Secret World of Female Gangsters

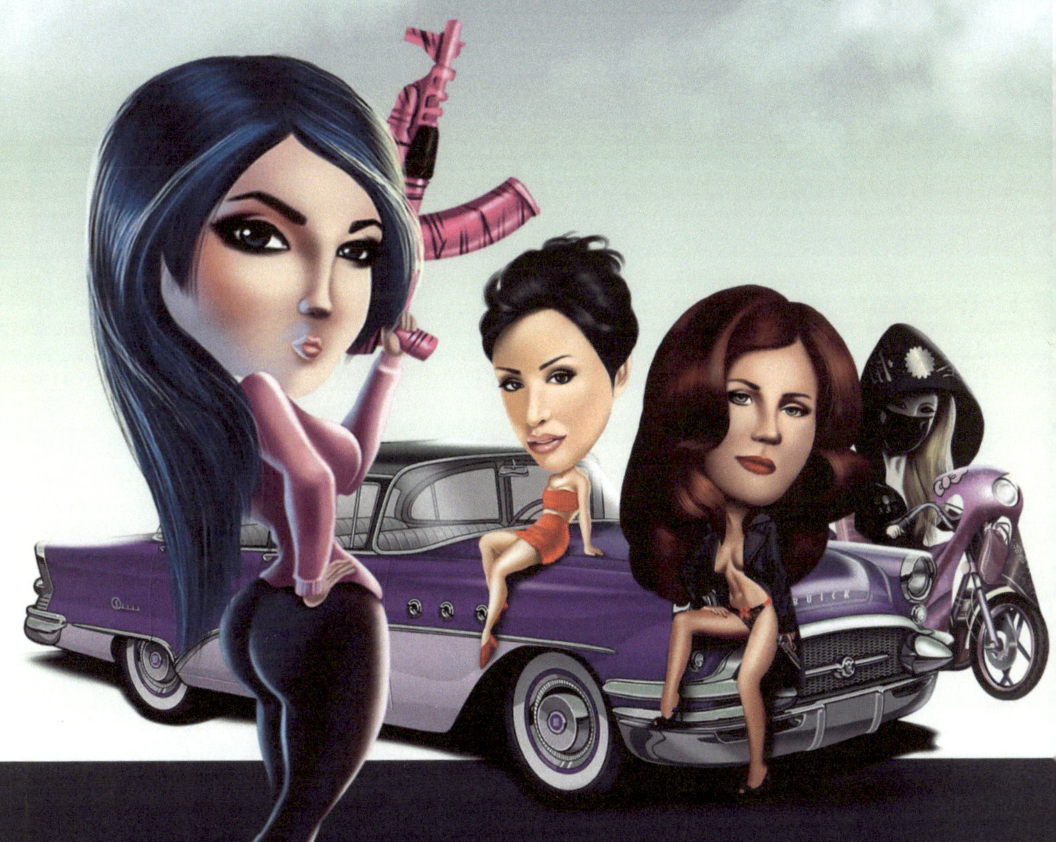

Written by Jerry Bader

Illustrated by Dream Computers

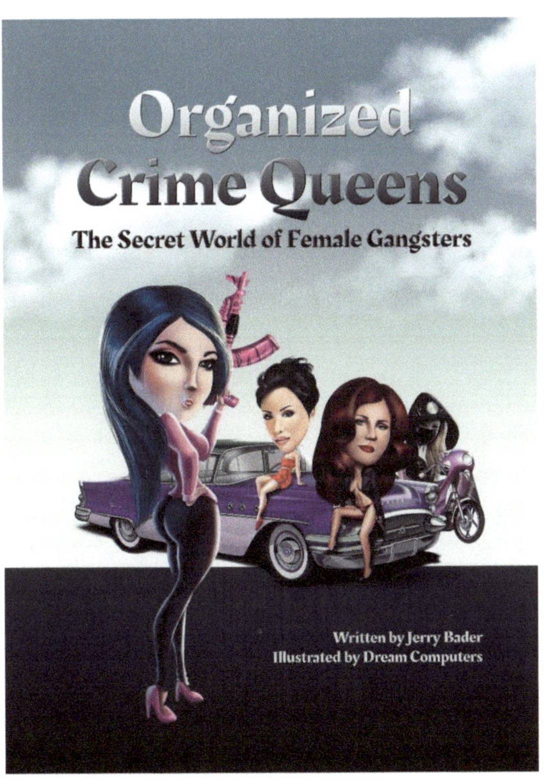

Written by Jerry Bader
Illustrations by Dream Computer

Produced by
MRPwebmedia.cm/books

The Secret World of Female Gangsters

Most of society thinks of women as the gentler sex, the sex with more compassion and empathy, not prone to violence. The truth is history and current events are littered with stories of violent women who do whatever it takes to get what they want; women who either revel in, or accept as needed, whatever acts of torture, murder and depravity that are required to achieve their goals.

We're not talking about mundane psychopaths that kill their children and their husbands, or homicidal maniacs that kill randomly without purpose, other than for some sexual or psychological gratification. We're talking about female organized crime bosses, leaders of highly structured, often successful criminal organizations.

Most everyone knows about the high profile male mobsters; people like Lucky Luciano, Myer Lansky, Bugsy Segal, Arnold Rothstein, and Al Capone: men who became legends, rightly or wrongly, due to the public's insatiable appetite for literature, movies, and television stories based on their lives. But what about their female counterparts, they definitely existed and still exist.

Their stories are both fascinating and cautionary. Their histories provide an alternative perspective on the equality of the sexes; everything has a price. We are talking about smart, capable, talented, ruthless women who under other circumstances might have become leaders in either business or politics; women who demanded respect, loyalty and a big payday; or else.

Forty Elephants
The Female Gang That Terrorized London

The idea of a gang of highly intelligent, dangerous, wild living, independent criminal women led by an extraordinary individual who thought she was the reincarnation of some Amazon Queen is unusual, if not unique. In today's society Alice Diamond might have become the CEO of a major multinational corporation, or perhaps the Prime Minister of England, but in the early twentieth century, ruthless women of ambition, strength, and intellect were not given access to the educational and leadership avenues available to men.

If there's a lesson to be learned from the tale of the Forty Elephants it's that denying access to opportunity based on bias, prejudice, or preconception will ultimately bite society in the ass, extracting a larger price than if opportunity was provided to all. On the other hand, there are individuals and groups of males and females who refuse to work within the confines of society to create change and prefer a self-indulgent, nihilistic pursuit of self-gratification and interest.

The Forty Elephants, also known as the Forty Thieves, were an all-female gang of criminals that operated in London from the 1700s up until the 1950s. They reached their heyday in the years between WWI and WWII under the leadership of twenty-year old Alice Diamond, also known as *Diamond Annie*, due to her penchant for wearing diamond rings that she often used as a weapon. More than one assailant lost an eye or suffered severe physical injury from one of her namesake fashion statements.

Alice Diamond
Queen of Thieves

At five feet, eight inches tall, Diamond was physically imposing with a hair-trigger temper, not afraid to use violence against anyone who got in her way, including the police, or even members of her own gang that didn't follow her rules. Alice and her girls dressed in the latest fashions presenting an attractive sophisticated facade to the world while at the same time enjoying wild parties and high living. Diamond had highly developed organizational skills and an understanding of how to take advantage of unfortunate women that suffered poor treatment by domineering male family members. She organized her gang in cells and developed a command structure that took advantage of her associates' particular talents. She herself was known as the *Queen of Thieves* handling the muscle, the overall organization, and what could be best described as the cultural and strategic vision of the group. She left much of the tactical planning to her second-in-command, Margaret Hughes, also known as *Baby Face Maggie Hill*, a woman who was particularly skilled at developing and implementing blackmail schemes.

The gang specialized in shoplifting, robbery, blackmail, and extortion. Although they had no official male members they often used men as getaway drivers using the new-fangled automobile to make their speedy getaways. They were also associated with the Elephant and Castle Gang, a male group that controlled much of the crime in West End London. Maggie Hill was the sister of well-known criminal Billy Hill who was responsible for planning the infamous 1952 Eastcastle Street postal van robbery and a significant 1954 bullion heist. All in all these women were well tapped into London's criminal underworld.

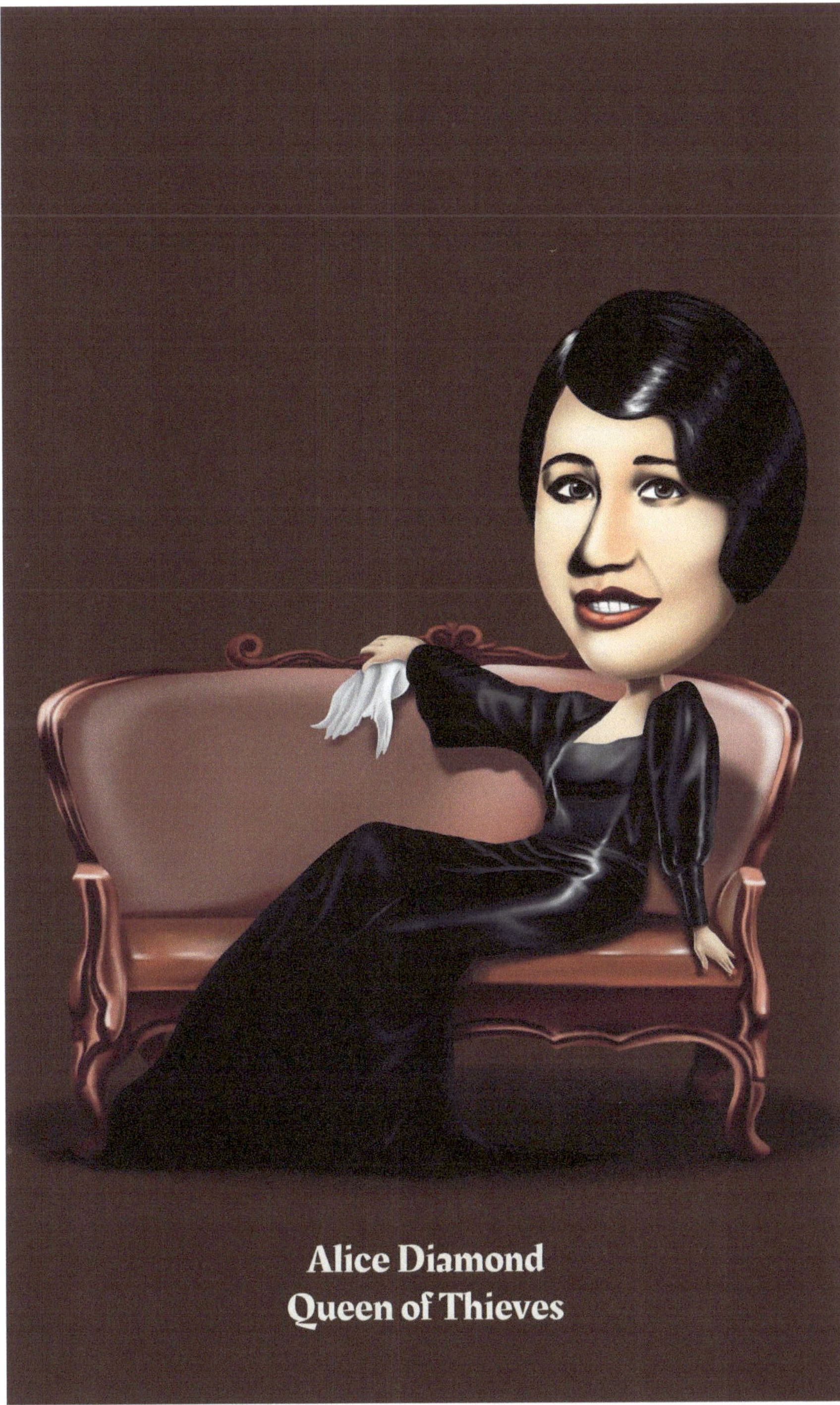

Alice Diamond
Queen of Thieves

The members of the Forty Elephants were attractive, disenfranchised women prone to aggression, drinking, and wild parties. They dressed stylishly in specially made clothes designed to hide the merchandise they stole from department stores. During the years between the wars women were regarded as the weaker sex and thus were not considered threats, something Diamond and her girls took every advantage of during their well-planned robbery assaults. In some cases, different groups of women would enter a department store like Selfridges from different entrances and create utter confusion by grabbing everything of value they could lay their hands on; they would then quickly exit through different doors to waiting getaway cars driven by their male accomplices.

Some of the women would get jobs in the homes of wealthy individuals in order to case the residence for valuables. The information would be passed on to Maggie Hill who would then plan a break-in. Other members of the gang targeted wealthy aristocrats for seduction and blackmail.

Diamond Annie's Downfall

In the end Diamond Annie was done-in by one of her own girls falling in love with an outsider, something that was forbidden. Maria Britten came from a good family and fell in love with a fellow called Jackson. Maria knew this was forbidden, so she went to Diamond with her father as protection, but Diamond flew into a rage and attacked Maria while Maggie Hill went after her father with a razor. Maria and her father managed to escape but that wasn't the end of it. Maria married Jackson the next day.

Several days later, a group from the Forty Elephants led by Diamond and Hill surrounded the Britten home. The women threw rocks and bottles through the windows; they entered the home determined to punish the wayward Britten and her family. The women found Mrs. Britten and her new baby in her bedroom. Mrs. Britten and the baby were forcefully thrown out of bed so their attackers could turn it over to see if Mr. Britten was hiding underneath. They eventually caught up with Britten and his son on the basement stairs and attacked them. The police finally showed up arresting several of the women that failed to escape. Mr. Britten and his son were taken to the hospital where Britten was patched up with twenty stitches. The police ultimately rounded up all the attackers.

Another account of the story goes slightly differently and perhaps more credibly. In this variation of events Maria Jackson, née Britten, attacked another woman, Bertha Tappenden, with a broken wine glass during a wild drinking party in 1925 at The Canterbury Arms Club in Waterloo, South London. Maria Britten must have already been married and she wasn't the sweet young thing made out in the alternative tale. During the drunken brawl Maria's father Bill Britten took a poke at Tappenden in an attempt to back up his daughter, causing an even bigger brouhaha. It was after Britten left that Alice Diamond and friends decided that Britten must be confronted. When Diamond knocked on Britten's door, she was greeted with a pail of water in the face, and that's when the full on attack on the Britten's house took place.

A trial was held but authorities were afraid that Diamond and Hill would release information on important members of the community that they'd acquired from the gang's seduction and extortion operations. As a result, the trial centered only on the house attack, rather than on the organization's broader criminal activities.

Diamond Alice and Baby-faced Maggie were both found guilty of the attack on the Britten's residence. They were sentenced to long prison terms of hard labor. With the leadership of the Forty Elephants in jail, the gang's fortunes declined. It remained in operation in one form or another up until the 1950s but never again did it reach the level of success it had under the ruthless guidance of Diamond Annie and Baby Face Maggie Hill. Alice Diamond survived her prison term and lived out her life in obscurity. She died sometime in the 1950s.

Maggie Hill fared far worse. In 1938 she was arrested for stabbing a policeman in the eye with a hatpin. On her release from jail the only work she could get was as a prostitute's maid and police informant, reporting on abusive pimps that the working girls feared. She evidently committed suicide sometime in the seventies but by that time the Forty Elephants had long since been relegated to history.

Aussie Prohibition
And the Rise of Sydney's Female Gangsters

Although indigenous Aboriginal peoples have been living in Australia for thousands of years and Europeans explored the continent in the 1600s, it wasn't until 1788 when the British decided to establish a penal colony on Botany Bay (Sydney) that Australia became what it is today. It's not surprising that a place that got its modern start in life by being colonized by petty criminals and political prisoners produced its share of gangsters.

The post WWI era produced some of the most interesting and inventive female Prohibition era gangsters. Nineteen twenties' Sydney had its lady crime bosses just like London. Sydney's distaff

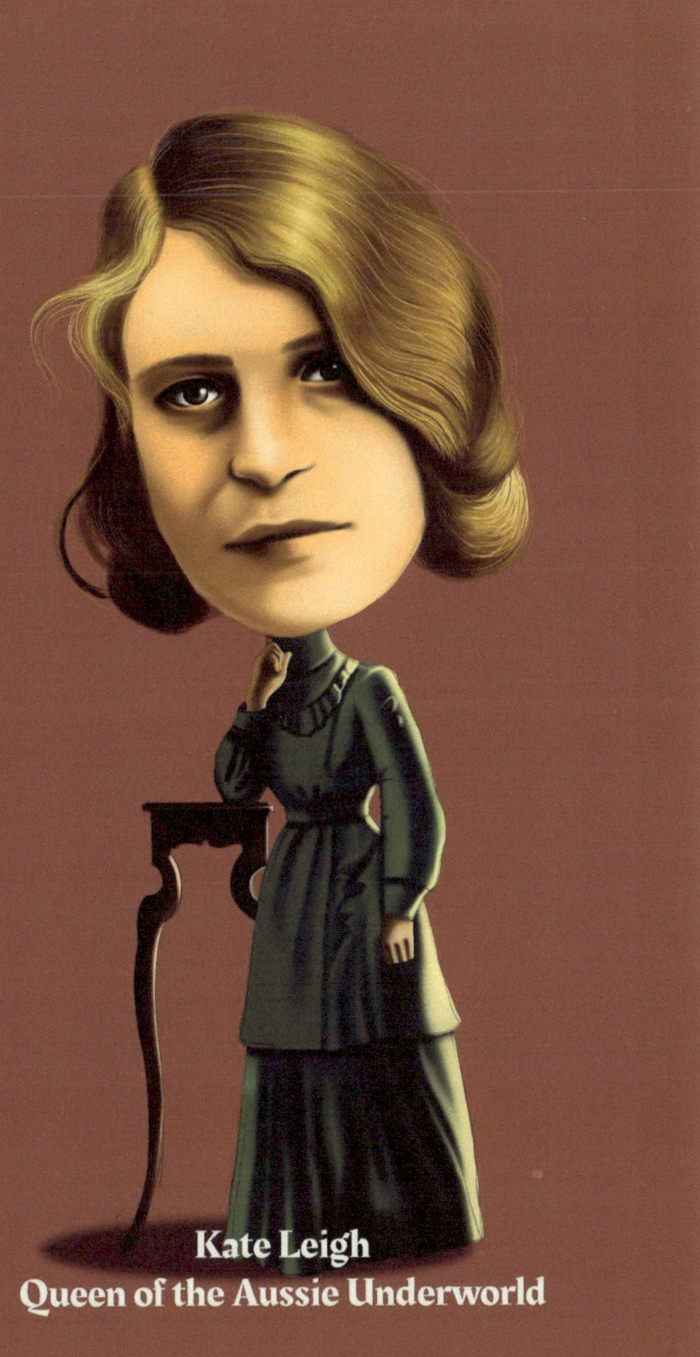

Kate Leigh

Queen of the Aussie Underworld

criminal scene was dominated by two vicious women each vying for power and control of the illegal liquor, prostitution, and drug businesses.

Kate Leigh
Queen of the Aussie Underworld

Catherine Mary Josephine "Kate" Leigh (née Beahan) was born in 1881. Leigh was born into a dysfunctional family, one of eight children to bookmaker Timothy Beahan and his wife Charlotte. Leigh was a neglected child that spent time in a home for girls and in 1900 had a child out-of-wedlock. At the height of her criminal career, her alcohol and cocaine businesses made her one of the richest women in Australia. Like London's Diamond Annie, Leigh had a fondness for diamond rings and often showed up in court with diamond rings on each of her fingers.

In 1902 Leigh married petty criminal and illegal bookmaker James Ernest 'Jack' Lee. Lee's father was Chinese and his mother was Australian. In 1905 Lee was jailed for robbery and assault. Kate was accused of being an accomplice in the assault as well as perjuring herself in an attempt to save her husband. She was convicted but the verdict was ultimately overturned. Kate and Lee separated after he was incarcerated but they did not officially divorce until 1921. She then anglicized Lee to Leigh, which she was known as for the rest of her life.

In 1922 she married a *sly-grog* dealer, Edward Joseph 'Teddy' Barry. *Sly-grog* was Australian slang for poor quality illegal alcohol, what Americans of the era might call 'bathtub gin.' The marriage didn't last. She lived with a series of men during the rest of the 1920s. One of these men was Wally Tomlinson, her bodyguard, a man with a violent past and a reputation as a dangerous *standover man,* Australian slang for an extortionist. She was married two more times, but marriage for Leigh seemed to be more of a working relationship with benefits rather than a match made in heaven.

Although she ran a series of brothels and was involved in the drug business, her main moneymaking operation revolved around the sale of illegal alcohol in numerous *sly-grog shops.* The Government, in an attempt to stop working men from getting drunk after work, mandated the hotel bars stop serving alcohol by 6 P.M. allowing workers only an hour to get drunk.

Like Prohibition in the U.S.A. it created a profitable opportunity for enterprising criminal entrepreneurs like Kate Leigh. Despite her career path and life choices, Leigh was known not to drink or smoke. The *Dangerous Drugs Amendment Act of 1927* also provided Leigh with the opportunity to establish a profitable cocaine distribution business delivered through a network of doctors, dentists, pharmacists, and sailors. Bad public policy has consequences; the quartet of ill-conceived laws passed in Australian around this time resulted in the creation of people like Leigh and her hated rival, Tilly Devine.

Of course Leigh wasn't the only one interested in profiting from the quartet of bad laws that included: The Dangerous Drugs (Amendment) Act of 1927, The Vagrancy Act NSW of 1905, The Betting and Gaming Act of 1906, and The Licensing Act of 1916 (NSW). These regulations attempted to outlaw or severely restrict the availability of drugs, prostitution, off-track betting, and alcohol, but of course all they really did was create a black market controlled by criminals. Leigh's main rival in these areas of opportunity was another female gangster and madam, Tilly Devine. Their legendary feuds during the twenties and thirties became known as the *Razor Gang Wars*, a name derived from the use of razors as the weapon of choice due to the passage of the Pistol Licensing Act (NSW) of 1927. Razors were cheap, easy to purchase, easy to hide, and deadly.

The Razor Gang Wars stretched from 1927 to 1930 reaching their pinnacle in 1929 resulting in two riots: the Battle of Blood Alley and the Battle of Kellett Street. Both Leigh and Devine were rumoured to be directly involved in these riots. Leigh had a loyal crew of male gangsters that protected her, but she was not shy at using a rifle to defend her turf. In 1930 she shot and killed John William 'Snowy' Prendergast after he broke into her home. She was also responsible for shooting Joseph McNamara but she was never indicted for either incident. Her luck eventually ran out when in 1930 the drug squad headed by famed Australian policewoman, Lillian Armfield raided one of her homes and found a quantity of cocaine. She was arrested, convicted, and sentenced to twelve months in jail. She was arrested a total of one hundred and seven times and sent to prison on thirteen of those occasions.

Violence is a fact of life when your business empire is based on the sale of illegal substances. The fact Leigh was a woman was irrelevant. She was surrounded by violence her whole life; her common-law husband and bodyguard, Henry George 'Jack' Baker was shot dead by John 'Chow' Hayes in front of their own house, a place used as her main sly-grog shop.

During the 1930s and 40s Leigh was one of the wealthiest woman in Australia. When she appeared in court she would show up in expensive clothes and diamond rings on every finger of both hands. Her financial decline was precipitated by the Tax Department that drove her into bankruptcy in 1954 for unpaid taxes dating back to 1942. In 1955, the illegal liquor business was all but snuffed out by a change in the law that allowed legal hotels to serve alcohol up until 10 P.M. The change in the law prompted Leigh to famously comment, *"The bloom has gone off the grog."* She died in 1964 at the age of 83 while living in poverty in a small room above one of her old properties supported by her nephew, William John Beahan, who worked out of the same building. Leigh is not only remembered for being one of the most colorful and wealthiest female Aussie criminals of the first half of the twentieth century, she is also remembered for her charitable acts during hard times.

Tilly Devine

Matilda 'Tilly' Devine, a madam and sly-grog distributor was Kate Leigh's main rival. During the Razor Wars it is rumored that the two actually came to blows during one of their many altercations. Tilly Devine was born in 1900 in London. She was the daughter of bricklayer Edward Twiss, a member of a prominent criminal family. By the age of fifteen she was working as a prostitute and thief. At sixteen she married an Australian serviceman, James Edward Devine, and promptly had a son the following year. She remained working as a prostitute even after she was married, resulting in numerous arrests and convictions for prostitution, theft, and assault. Tilly followed her husband back to Australia leaving her son behind to be raised by her parents. After arriving in Australia Tilly continued her career as a prostitute, and along with her husband started dealing drugs.

Devine quickly graduated to brothel owner. The NSW Vagrancy Act of 1905 prohibited men from running brothels opening the door for enterprising women like Devine. Along with running the brothel, Devine organized a gang to protect her operation from rivals, and she paid off the police in order to avoid prosecution. Historian Larry Writer describes Devine's clever pimping hierarchy: people of prominence like politicians and wealthy businessmen were serviced by the elite *call girls*; *tenement girls* working to supplement their incomes or addictions, serviced the next rung down on the social ladder; while older hookers called, *boat girls*, targeted the sailors and working class.

Like Leigh, Devine became a wealthy woman living the good life. She owned property, expensive automobiles, and substantial amounts of gold and diamond jewellery. Her wealth was considerable even after the cost of bribes to the police and fines to the court for her multiple convictions. Her career lasted fifty years racking up two hundred and four convictions. She spent numerous stretches in jail for various offences including: prostitution, assault, affray (public disturbance), and attempted murder.

Jim Devine, her violent alcoholic husband, specialized in extortion with convictions for theft, pimping, and drug dealing. He was also a murderer, gunning down fellow criminal Gregory Gaffney and aiding infamous hit man, Frankie Green in the murder of former rugby player, Barney Dalton, an associate of Kate Leigh during the Razor Gang Wars. He also accidentally killed taxi driver, Frederick Herbert Moffitt. Although he was arrested and charged with murder for both the Gaffney and Moffitt killings, he managed to escape conviction by pleading self-defence. His violent nature overlapped into his marriage. On one occasion he tried to shoot Tilly but she

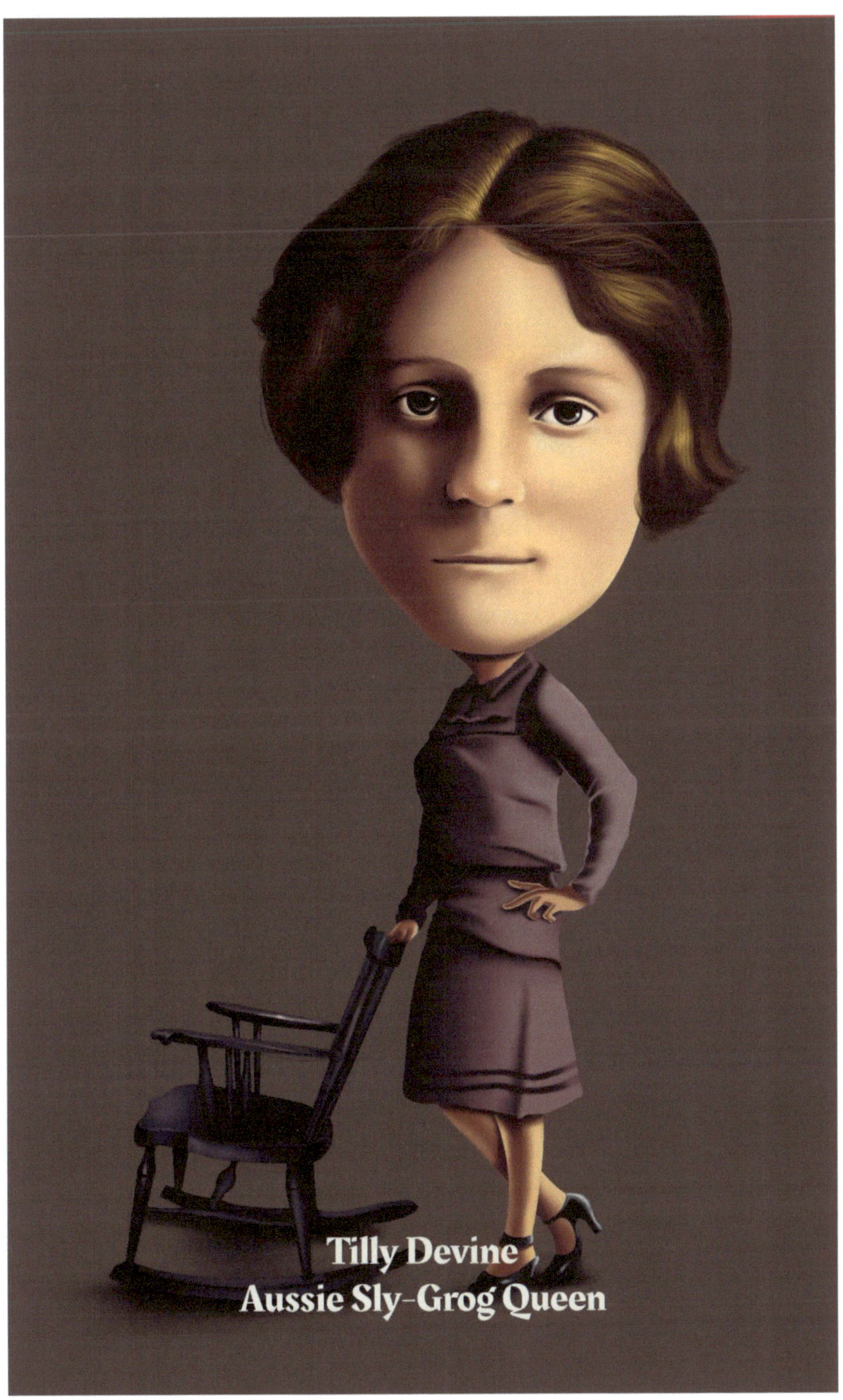

Tilly Devine
Aussie Sly-Grog Queen

managed to escape the house unharmed. The neighbours called the police and he was arrested but never convicted as Tilly refused to testify.

She put up with Devine until 1940 when they separated and by 1944 they were divorced. She then took up with another thug, Skinny Kenny, also an extortionist or stand-over man. In 1945 she married Eric John Parsons but before she did, she shot him in the leg. She was arrested for the shooting but was acquitted. One could say, it was love at first-shot. They remained married for thirteen years until Parsons died of cancer in 1958. Like Leigh her decline was the result of tax evasion. In 1955 the Tax Department ordered her to pay £20,000 in back taxes and fines resulting in her having to declare bankruptcy. She managed to stay in business until 1968 when she sold off her last remaining brothel. She died two years later at the age of seventy.

Stephanie St. Clair
Queenie

Stephanie, *Queenie*, St. Clair, also known simply as Madame St. Clair, was born in 1886 either in Martinique of French and African descent, or in Guadalupe Island off the coast of Mexico. She moved from Marseille in Southern France to Harlem in 1912, and by 1922 she parlayed ten thousand dollars of her own money into a thriving numbers operation. For muscle, she initially aligned herself with a gang of Irish thugs called the *Forty Thieves*, not to be confused with London's all-girl Forty Elephants that was also known as the Forty Thieves. Eventually she formed her own strongarm muscle, headed by future gangster legend, Ellsworth, *Bumpy*, Johnson.

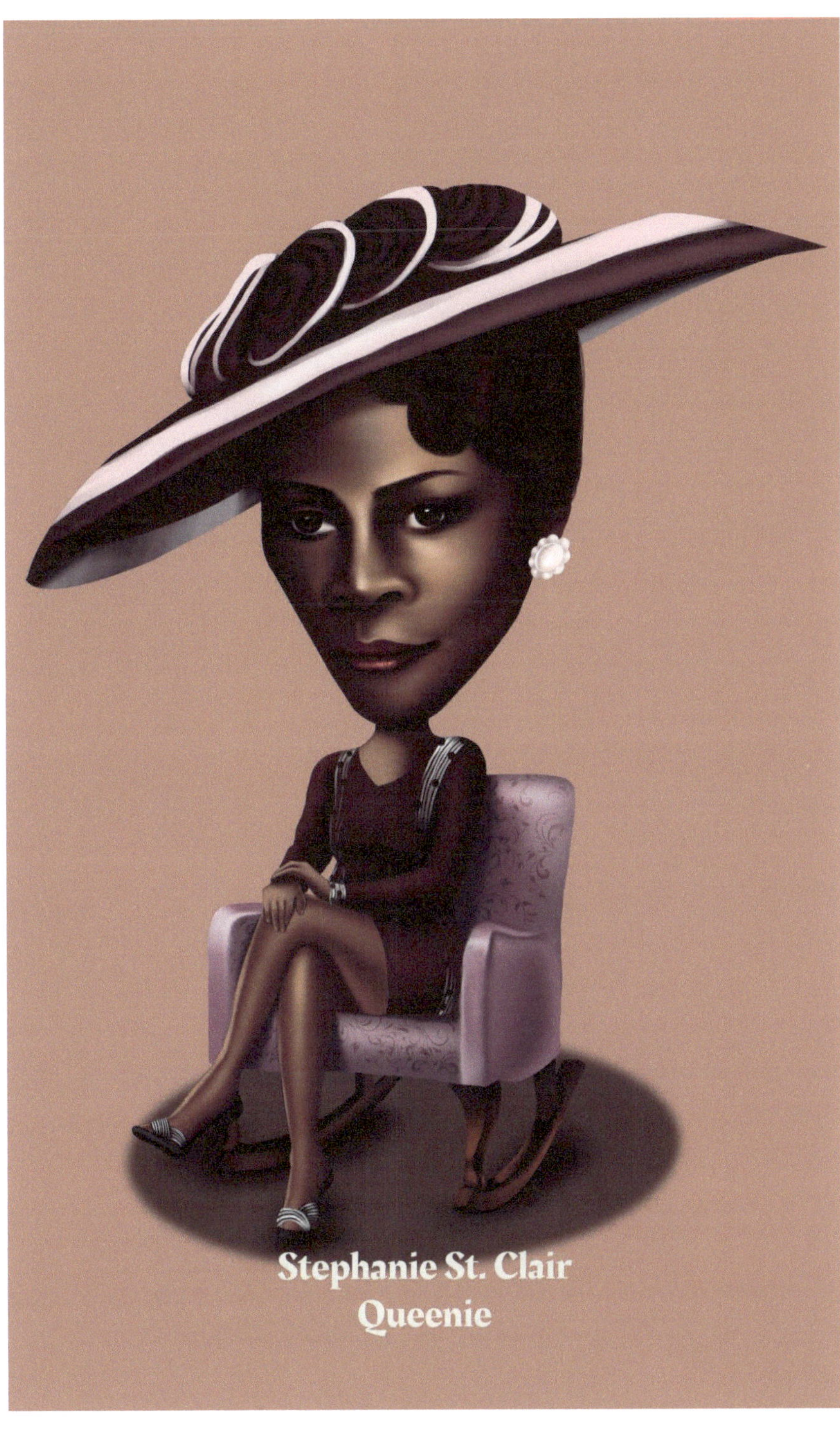

Stephanie St. Clair
Queenie

It didn't take *Queenie* long to build an organization of fifty people bringing in an estimated two hundred thousand dollars a year, the equivalent of over six million dollars today. Her numbers racket was so profitable both the Italian and Jewish gangs wanted a piece of the action. Even the police she was paying off for protection wanted a bigger share. After the cops ignored her complaints about harassment she took out ads in the local Harlem newspapers accusing the police of corruption. She was promptly arrested on false charges. She got even when it came time for her to testify in front of the Seabury Commission by testifying about her payoffs to police officials resulting in twelve policemen being fired.

Dutch Schultz was the most aggressive Mafia figure intent on taking over *Queenie's* action. Schultz's crew either beat or killed any of *Queenie's* people who didn't pay him protection. Forty people were killed in the war between Schultz and *Queenie*.

Queenie refused to give in to Schultz but the violence was getting out of hand so she ordered her enforcer, *Bumpy* Johnson, to go over Schultz's head and cut a deal with Lucky Luciano, head of the Mafia Commission. Of course *Bumpy* also negotiated for a piece of the action for himself. The deal laid the groundwork for Johnson's rise in status, as he became the main contact between the Mafia and the Harlem underworld. Eventually Johnson would earn the title, *Harlem's Godfather*. Schultz became a problem for Luciano and the five New York families that formed The Commission, As Mafia leader, Luciano ordered Schultz killed. He was assassinated in 1935.

Stephanie St. Clair eventually retired a rich woman leaving *Bumpy* in charge of the criminal empire they built. She died in 1969.

Gertrude Lythgoe
The Bahama Queen

The Prohibition Era is filled with stories of smugglers, bootleggers, and the rise of organized crime, most of which revolves around the exploits of well-known male criminals who achieved legendary status with their life stories recreated in just about every form of media available including: print, broadcast, and digital. But the history of Prohibition America would not be complete without a discussion of an exotic beauty with brains and guts; a woman the press dubbed *The Bahama Queen*. During the early 1920s Gertrude Lythgoe was probably the most successful smuggler of whiskey into the United States from the British owned Bahamas.

Unlike many of the female criminals of the modern era, that are violent, crude, and often reckless, Gertrude Lythgoe was refined, well-spoken, and sophisticated, with a strong head for business and a resolve that would not tolerate any perceived slight. Lythgoe was born in Ohio, one of ten children to an English father and Scottish mother. As she grew into an adult her exotic beauty gave rise to her first nickname, *Cleo*, after the legendary Cleopatra. She lived in New York and California finding work as a stenographer, eventually finding employment with the Haig and McTavish Scotch whiskey company. The legal importation of liquor stopped with the passing of the 1919 Volstead Act, banning the sale and consumption of alcohol in the United States. Not surprisingly in a climate similar to today's marijuana prohibition, doctors earned some forty million dollars writing whiskey prescriptions, while the abuse of the religious sacramental exception was substantial.

Lythgoe's employer recognized her business talents so she was given the job of setting up a legal distribution operation in Nassau, Bahamas. Her independence insulated the company from prosecution while at the same time provided the ambitious Lythgoe with a profitable business opportunity. She was the only woman at this time to have a wholesale liquor license in the Bahamas, a place that still had a reputation as a haven for ne'er-do-wells, modern-day buccaneers, and scoundrels. She rented a warehouse for the whiskey and a room at the Lucerne Hotel: ground zero for bootleggers, adventurers, and characters of all types. A psychiatric nurse named Dorothy Donnelle, who was affectionately known as *Mother* ran the hotel.

Prior to Prohibition in 1917, fifty thousand quarts of liquor were shipped to the United States; by 1922 that amount had risen to ten million, and Gertrude Lythgoe was responsible for much of it, with the help of shipbuilder and gentlemen smuggler Bill McCoy, whose interest in Gertrude was more than mere profiteering. McCoy was an honest, sober criminal that could be trusted to do what he promised, hence the expression, *the real McCoy*. Lythgoe would occasionally accompany McCoy on his runs to make sure everything ran smoothly. The two friends became close, although they never ended up together despite McCoy's well-intentioned efforts.

McCoy would sail to just outside the U.S. three-mile limit in an area called *Rum Row*, a name derived from the large number of vessels waiting for customers to pick up their alcohol shipments that would then be smuggled into the United States. Eventually the three-mile limit was extended to twelve miles in 1924.

Lythgoe was not only a shrewd and accomplished businesswoman; she was also not one to be trifled with. When a competitor

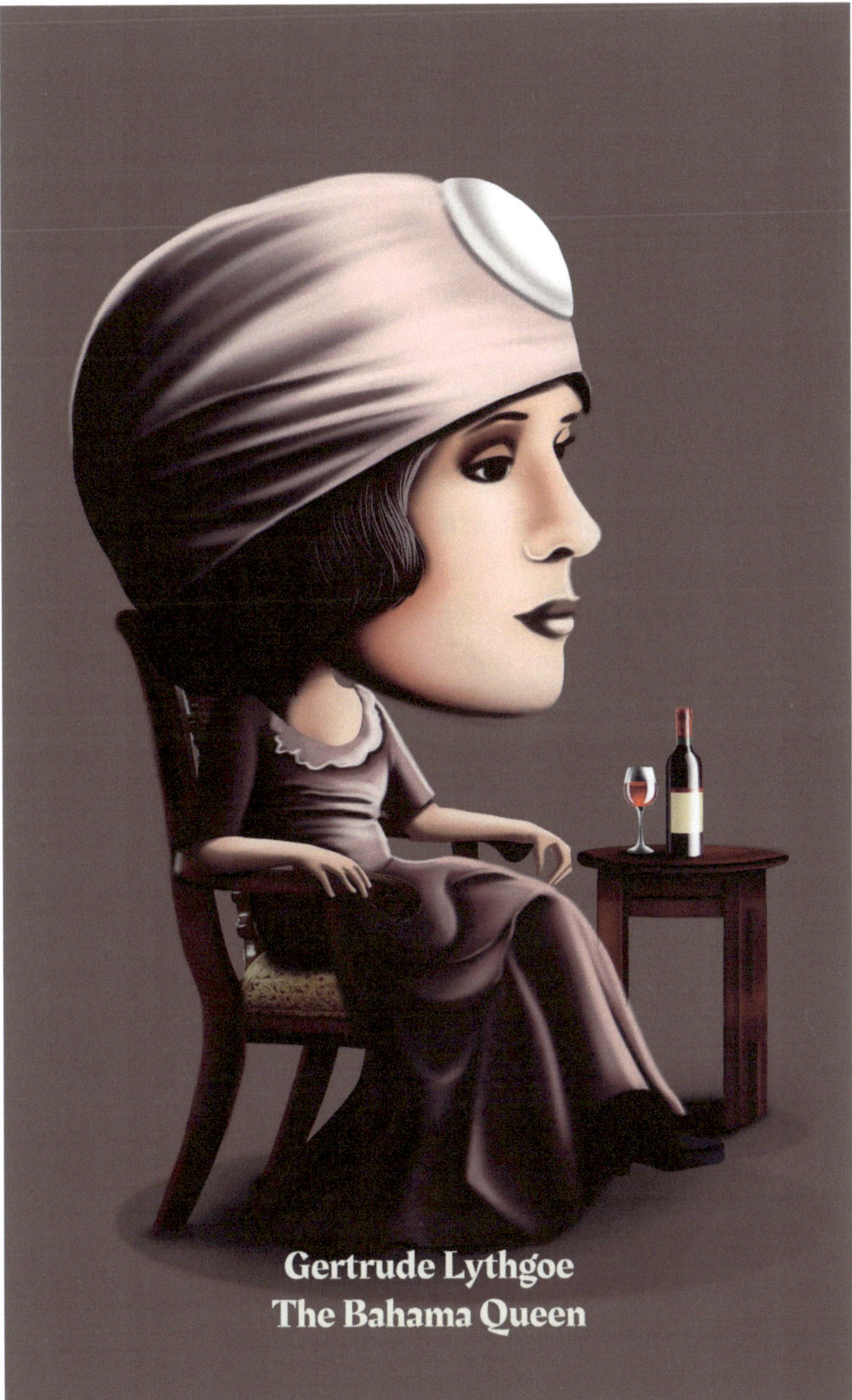

Gertrude Lythgoe
The Bahama Queen

disparaged her product and her reputation, she took action. She confronted the slanderer while he sat in a barber's chair having a shave. She demanded he accompany her to her office where she promptly threatened to put a bullet in him if he didn't change his slanderous behaviour.

She was ultimately arrested for trying to smuggle whiskey into New Orleans but was cleared of the charges when it was proven she was elsewhere when the crime was committed. If legal business opportunities would have been available to her during this era she could have been a very successful legitimate business leader, which she eventually did become after her retirement from the bootlegging business sometime in the mid 1920s. After retiring she found her way to Miami, New York, and then Detroit where she spent twenty-five years building a fortune in the fledgling car rental business. Eventually she moved to Los Angeles where she died in 1974 at the age of eighty-six. At the time of her death she was worth millions of dollars.

Prohibition was a social, economic, and cultural disaster resulting in the rise of organized crime, a lesson that does not appear to have ever been learned based on the still existing underclass that finds the illegal drug business a solution to poverty and lack of opportunity.

Being a beautiful, smart, well-spoken, sophisticated woman in a man's world of adventure, smuggling, and murder made Gertrude Lythgoe the perfect subject for numerous newspaper stories in the New York Times, Los Angeles Times, and the Chicago Tribune. She is truly a legend and in many ways a feminist success.

Marie Waite
Spanish Marie

Gertrude Lythgoe wasn't the only female rum and whiskey-runner of the Prohibition Era. Another legendary figure that had her own fleet of fast moving, rum-ladened ships was Marie Waite, the six-foot tall, blue-eyed, black-haired, hot-tempered siren who disposed of lovers as easily as she unloaded her cargoes of illegal booze. Marie's career started in earnest after the death of her husband Charlie Waite, *"king of the rum runners"* a title that may have been disputed by people like Bill McCoy who was probably just as happy to have someone else wear the mantle while he continued quietly delivering his cargos of liquid gold. After Charlie was killed by the Coast Guard in a shootout on Biscayne Bay in 1926, Marie decided she should continue the family business; after all, a girl's got to earn a living, and rum running was the family stock and trade.

Like Lythgoe, Marie Waite was a sharp businesswoman but instead of setting up shop in the Bahamas, Marie opted for Havana, Cuba as the perfect location for her headquarters; a location that featured an unlimited supply of rum, and conveniently located close to Key West and Palm Beach. Unlike Lythgoe who used the transportation services of Bill McCoy, *Spanish Marie*, as she became known, preferred her own fleet of fast moving ships, what in today's business jargon we'd call vertical integration. Not only was she strategically clever, she had a good head for tactics. Her delivery system featured four ships, three containing the booze, while the fourth functioned as an escort gunboat used to fight off any Coast Guard interference that got in their way.

Eventually the Coast Guard acquired faster ships able to catch up to Marie's fleet. Not to be outdone our clever girl went high tech on the Coast Guard by setting up an unlicensed radio transmitting station on Key West and equipping all her ships with radios so they could communicate. She even developed a code system in Spanish just in case the messages were intercepted; but the Coast Guard eventually figured out how her code worked.

In 1928 the jig was up when she was arrested in Coconut Grove, Miami along with her crew while unloading a shipment of rum, whiskey, gin, champagne, and beer. She was released on a five-hundred-dollar bond after pleading she had to look after her two small children. When she didn't show-up the next day, the judge ordered the bond be increased to three thousand dollars but that didn't faze Spanish Marie. The following day she was nowhere to be found, but her attorney did show-up in court asking for a continuance. The attorney said Marie was in bed with severe depression and anxiety caused by the arrest. Since the lawyer didn't get a doctor's certificate attesting to Marie's anxiety, the continuance was denied. The whole charade provided enough time for Marie to make her getaway. So instead of going to jail, Marie, her boats, and her money disappeared, never to be seen or heard from again; a fitting end to the legend of Spanish Marie Waite.

Laura Bullion
The Thorny Rose

The post-Civil War era was known for numerous outlaw gangs including the well-known Wild Bunch led by Butch Cassidy. The gang was made famous by the movie, *Butch Cassidy and the Sundance Kid* (1969); it operated out of Hole-In-The Wall, Wyoming, and is

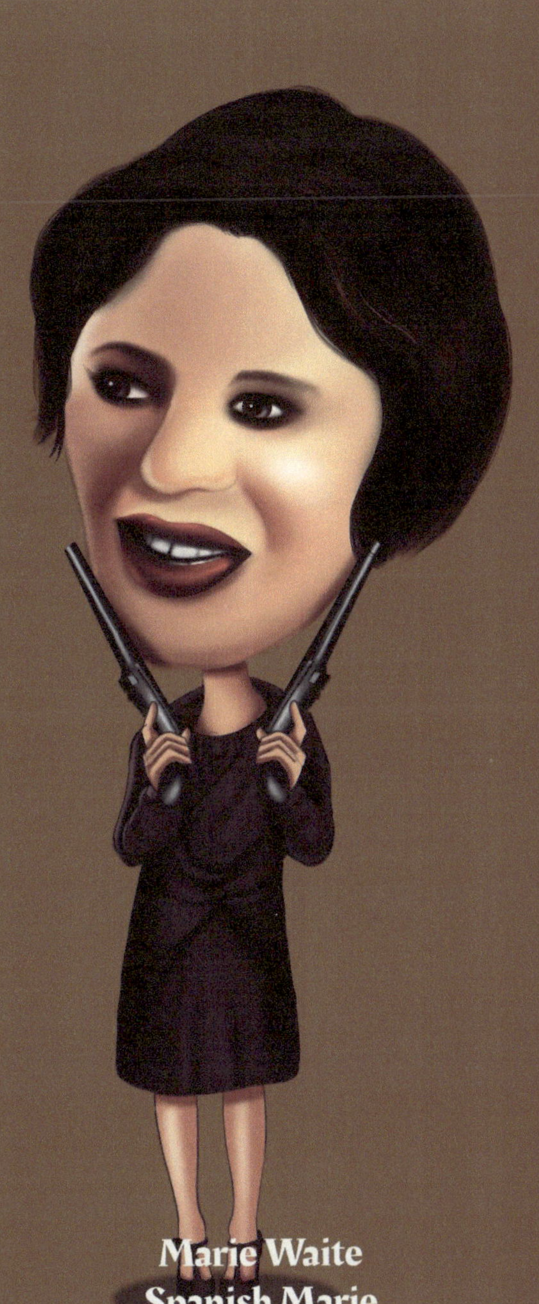

Marie Waite
Spanish Marie

sometimes referred to as The Hole-In-The-Wall Gang. Amongst the gang's members were the *Sundance Kid* (Harry Alonzo Longabaugh), *Black Jack* Ketchum, *Kid* Curry Logan, *Flat-Nose* George Curry, Ben *The Tall Texan* Kilpatrick, and William *News* Carver, nicknamed *News* because of his fondness for seeing his name in the newspaper. Amongst the male members of the gang was, a sometime prostitute and fellow outlaw, Laura Bullion. Bullion wasn't the only female outlaw associated with the group. Ann and Josie Bassett were also closely connected to the gang.

Laura Bullion's early life is a bit of a muddled blur. She may have been born in Knickerbocker, Texas, sometime in 1876, probably in October. She may also have been born in Conway, Arkansas, or maybe somewhere in Kentucky in 1873. What we do know is her mother, Fereby Byler was German, and her outlaw father, Henry Bullion was Native American. Henry was an acquaintance of Wild Bunch gang members, William *News* Carver and Ben *The Tall Texan* Kilpatrick, both of whom Laura met when she was just thirteen. Laura worked as a prostitute up until she was sixteen or seventeen, and then occasionally afterward, mostly at Madame Fannie Porter's whorehouse in San Antonio, Texas, a place frequented by the Wild Bunch crew.

Carver married Laura's aunt but she died soon after. He then had a relationship with the female rancher and outlaw, Josie Bassett, sister to Butch Cassidy's sometime girlfriend, Ann Bassett.

Carver then became romantically involved with Laura who later was involved with Ben *The Tall Texan* Kilpatrick after Carver became involved with another of Fannie Porter's girls Lillie Davis. The romantic relationships among the Wild Bunch men and Fannie

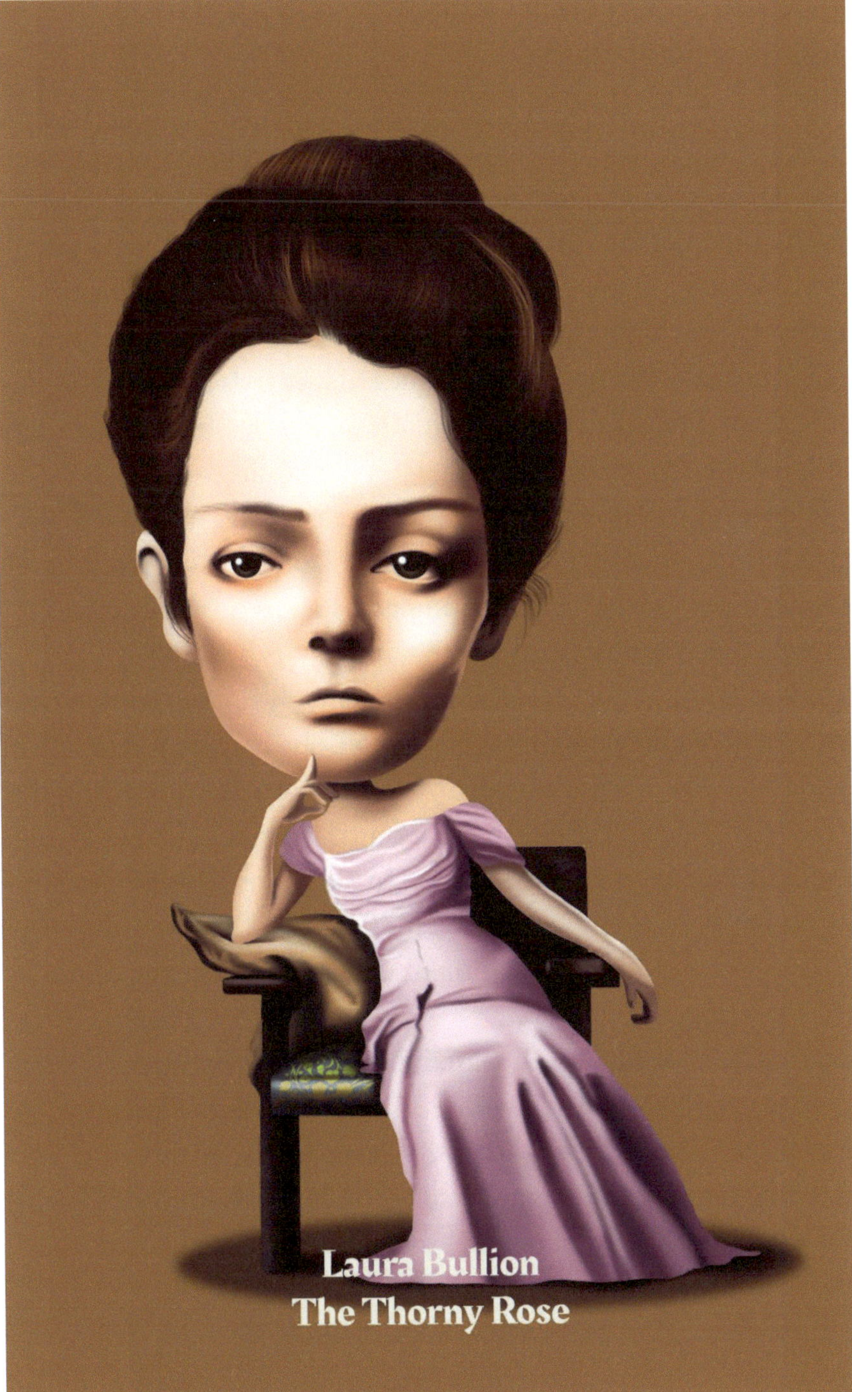
Laura Bullion
The Thorny Rose

Porter's girls seemed to be in perpetual flux, most likely a matter of convenience and availability.

During the 1890s Laura became directly involved in the Wild Bunch gang's operations, and not just as a companion, but also as an active participating member. In 1901 she was arrested and convicted for her involvement in the Great Northern train robbery. She was released after serving three and a half years. The gang gave Laura the nicknamed *Della Rose* after she met Kid Curry's girlfriend Della Moore. They also called her *Rose of the Wild Bunch*. She used a variety of aliases over the years including, Mrs. Benjamin Arnold, Mrs. Nellie Rose, Clara Hayes, Clara Casey, Desert Rose, and even Wild Bunch Rose. Newspaper reports on her arrest state she might have been disguised as a boy when taking part in a train robbery in Montana. She was described in the same report by Chief of Detectives Desmond as: "cool, shows absolutely no fear, and in male attire would readily pass for a boy." In 1918 she reappeared in Memphis as Mrs. Maurice Lincoln, a Civil War widow. In Memphis she made a living as a seamstress amongst a variety of other similar jobs. She died on December 2nd, 1961 in Memphis. The epitaph on her grave refers to her by yet another of her Wild Bunch nicknames, *The Thorny Rose*, no doubt a comment on her prickly personality.

As one of the handful of female members of the Wild Bunch, Laura Bullion was well acquainted with the mysterious Etta Place, the girlfriend of fellow gang member the *Sundance Kid*. Most of the Wild Bunch members were ultimately killed while involved in various robbery attempts and shootouts, except maybe Butch Cassidy and the *Sundance Kid*. The 1969 movie that made them famous purports that they were both killed in Bolivia by the Bolivian army; police reports state that they committed suicide after being fatally wounded; however, that may not be what actually happened. Curiously Etta Place disappeared around 1909 after returning from South America with the *Sundance Kid* (Harry Longabaugh) who supposedly returned to Bolivia to re-join his pal Butch Cassidy. At around the same time a woman named Eunice Gray, who was rumoured to actually be Etta Place, opened a brothel in Texas. Only Laura Bullion and the Bassett sisters would have known what actually happen to the famous trio, Butch Cassidy, the Sundance Kid, and Etta Place. In a 1960 interview Josie Bassett stated that Cassidy came to visit her in the 1920s and that he lived under the name of Johnnie Nevada until 1945. Josie Bassett died in 1964.

Ann Bassett
Queen Ann

Of the five women who were associated with the Wild Bunch the most interesting is rancher, outlaw, and all around Wild Bunch party girl Ann Bassett, the younger sister of Josie Bassett and daughter to Herb and Elizabeth Chamberlain Bassett. Born in Browns Park, Colorado in 1878 and raised in Utah, Ann and her sister, Josie were both attractive, well-educated tomboys, perfectly at home working on, and dealing with, the rough and often dangerous daily operations of a ranch. Both girls were what could best be described as sexually promiscuous having multiple affairs with several of the more prominent members of Butch Cassidy's Wild Bunch gang.

Herb Bassett operated a profitable cattle ranch located with easy access to Utah, Wyoming, and Colorado. His business included supplying the Wild Bunch with fresh horses and supplies when they needed them, mostly when they were on the run from the law.

Outlaws like Cassidy, *Kid Curry* Logan, and *Black Jack* Ketchum were amongst the frequent visitors to the ranch as the area was on the route used to move stolen horses and cattle. By the time Ann was fifteen she was having an affair with Butch Cassidy, while her sister Josie was sleeping with Cassidy's best friend, Elzy Lay. The relationships didn't seem to be exclusive as the girls also were involved with other members of the gang including Ben Kilpatrick and Will *News* Carver.

The sisters' ongoing sexual liaisons and friendship with members of the Wild Bunch provided them with hardened outlaw allies to help defend their property from the advances of local cattle barons determined to take over the Bassett ranch. The animosity between the Bassetts and the cattlemen increased with a tit-for-tat cattle-rustling war with each party accusing the other of stealing. The cattlemen went so far as to hire famed gunslinger Tom Horn to get the sisters to sell. Horn left the Bassett sisters alone, although he did go after and kill a number of other rustlers that had little or nothing to do with the sisters' activities. The sisters' involvement with the often-violent members of the Wild Bunch was enough to warn off anyone looking to harm the two women, including Horn.

Ann and Josie managed to sexually work their way through most of the members of the Wild Bunch without any apparent signs of animosity or jealously. The security these ever evolving sexual relationships provided could have been motivated by mere availability, but more likely they were a well-thought-out defensive strategy. Whatever the motivation, the Bassett sisters were two of only five women that were let into the Wild Bunch inner circle. In addition to Ann and Josie Bassett these women were the *Sundance Kid's* girlfriend Etta Place, Elzy Lay's future wife Maude Davis, and

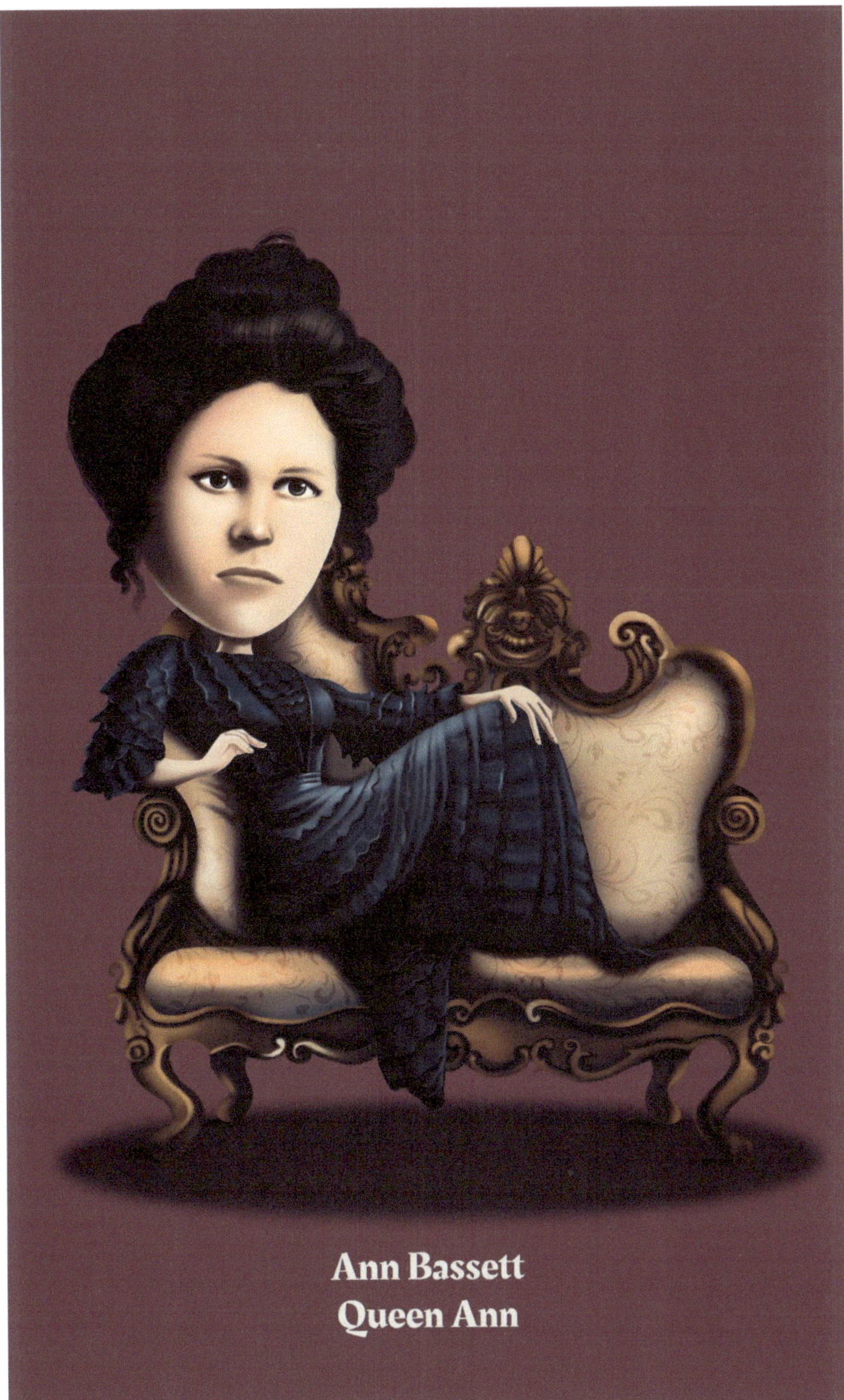

Ann Bassett
Queen Ann

gang member Laura Bullion. These were the only women the gang trusted enough to take to their Robber's Roost hideout. Butch Cassidy and Ann Bassett's on-again off-again relationship lasted seven years, often interrupted by Cassidy's bank and train robbing activities.

In 1903 Ann Bassett married Henry Bernard. The relationship lasted six years ending in divorce. After Cassidy escaped to South America she supposedly never saw him again. By 1904 most of the Wild Bunch were either dead or in prison. In 1928 Ann Bassett married again to cattleman Frank Willis. Their relationship lasted for the rest of her life. She died in 1956 at the age of seventy-seven. She requested that she be cremated and her ashes dispersed in her northern Utah hometown. In a macabre twist, Willis who really loved Bassett, couldn't bring himself to let go of the ashes. He carried them around in his car until his death in 1963. After he died, friends and family completed her wishes by burying her ashes in Browns Park.

Of course that can't be the end of the Ann Bassett story because like almost everything else associated with the legendary *Butch Cassidy* and *Sundance Kid*, things never were as simple as they appeared. There is speculation that Ann Bassett and the *Sundance Kid's* long-time girlfriend, the ever-elusive Etta Place, were actually the same person. Etta Place seems to have disappeared sometime around 1909. The speculation states that Bassett led a double life, simultaneously having affairs with Butch Cassidy as Ann Bassett, and the *Sundance Kid* as Etta Place. This idea might not be as crazy as it sounds based on the sexual history of the women involved with the gang. What makes it even more bizarre is that both men were apparently aware of it. Reports by the Pinkerton Detective Agency described both women in almost exactly the same way: classic good looks, articulate in speech, and intelligent. Both women had the same color hair and were proficient riding horses, shooting rifles, and promiscuous with multiple lovers. Comparisons of legitimate documented photographs of the two women reveal that they could easily be the same woman. They both have similar features, hair color, and overall physical appearance.

Dr. Thomas G. Kyle of the Computer Research Group at the Los Alamos National Laboratory, known for his work for various government intelligence agencies, concluded after analysis of the comparison photographs that their features matched, that both had the same scar or cowlick at the top of their foreheads, and that they appeared by all evidence to be the same woman. On the contrary there is evidence that Bassett was in the U.S. while Place was supposedly in South America, but who knows for sure.

Meanwhile Ann's sister, Josie, lived until 1963 when she died at the age of ninety after breaking her hip when a horse knocked her down.

Griselda Blanco
La Madrina

Every list of infamous female criminals seems to either begin or end with Griselda Blanco, *La Madrina,* or if you prefer *The Godmother.* Her reputation for violence and mayhem was so considerable that one nickname wasn't enough for arguably the most violent woman gangster of all time. She was variously referred to as the *Queen of Cocaine* for her criminal business activities and the *Black Widow* for her habit of killing her husbands.

She's responsible for the death of three of her spouses; she personally gunned down husband Alberto Bravo and six of his bodyguards with an Uzi submachine gun in a Bogotá parking lot. It was her way of negotiating a family dispute over some missing funds. But she didn't stop at killing just family, her death count started at age eleven when she killed a young boy whose parents refused to pay a kidnap ransom; and the death toll escalated to around two hundred and fifty by the time she herself was killed exiting a butcher shop in Colombia in 2012.

She started in the drug trade at age fourteen and by the time she was forty she was pushing three hundred kilos of cocaine per month, netting a cool eighty million dollars. She was arrested and jailed in Miami in 1985 for three murders but was released in 2004 over a legal technicality. Upon her release she was promptly deported back to Colombia. Her association with the Medellin cartel soured after she killed Marta Saldarriaga Ochoa in order to avoid paying for a shipment of cocaine. This time Blanco went too far. Marta was a niece to one of the Ochoa's who ran the Medellin Cartel. After that deadly blunder she was living on borrowed time. She managed to stay alive until 2012 when she was gunned down in the street by a drive-by motorcycle hit.

Sandra Avila Beltrán
La Reina del Pacífico

It seems that organized crime like real estate is all about three things: location, location, and location. In order to smuggle booze into the United States during Prohibition, rumrunners had to find

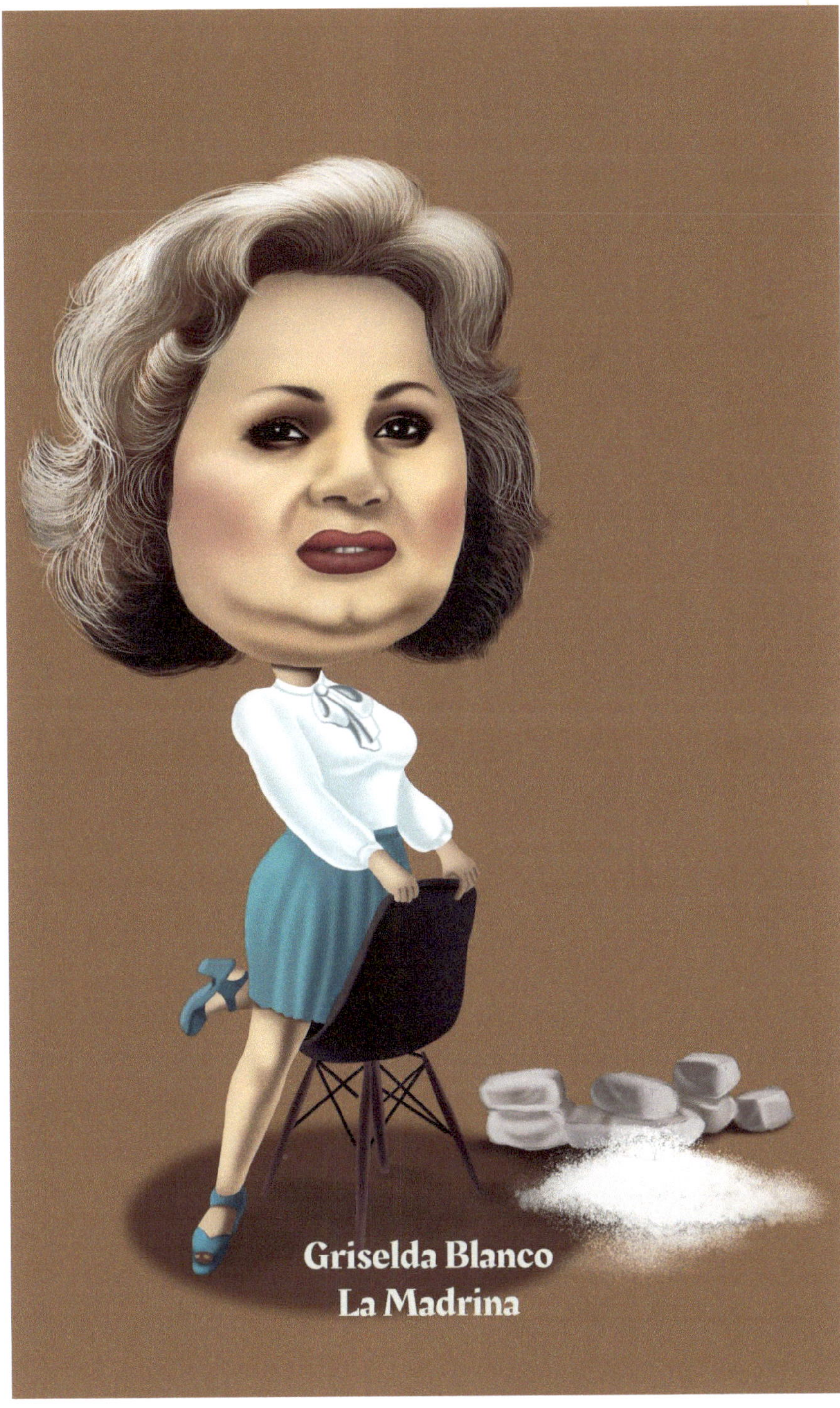

Griselda Blanco
La Madrina

friendly environments from where they could operate without too much government interference. Gertrude Lythgoe set up her operation in the Bahamas, while Marie Waite setup in Cuba. Alcohol also came into the United States from the booze-friendly confines of Canada. The days of alcohol Prohibition are long past; the distilleries that supplied the bootleggers, rumrunners, and smugglers of yesteryear are either long gone or established multinational corporations.

Today's illicit vice of choice is drugs and the hotbed locations for these operations are Colombia and Mexico. In the 1980s Griselda Blanco was the Queen of Colombian Cocaine distribution in Miami until her greed, fondness for violence, and stupidity caught up to her. Killing a member of the Ochoa family that ran the Colombian Medellin Cartel was not a smart move, and it ultimately got her killed. More recently we have another crime queen, this time from Mexico, but also with deep Colombian connections, *La Reina del Pacifico*, *The Queen of the Pacific*, Sandra Avila Beltrán.

Beltrán a third generation drug dealer was born in 1960 with deep family roots in the drug business. Her father is related to Rafael Caro Quintero, a former big shot in the Guadalajara Cartel. Her uncle is Miguel Angel Felix Gallardo, *El Padrino*, *The Godfather*, founder of the Guadalajara Cartel that controlled most of the drug traffic along the U.S. Mexican border. Gallardo was connected to the Colombian drug cartels, and insulated by his association with the Mexican DFS, *Direccion Federal de Seguirdad*, and the U.S. CIA. Gallardo is currently serving a forty-year prison sentence for killing Enrique Camarena, a U.S. DEA agent. Beltran's mother's family was just as connected. They were deeply involved in heroin smuggling during the 1970s, moving up, or down as the case maybe, to cocaine

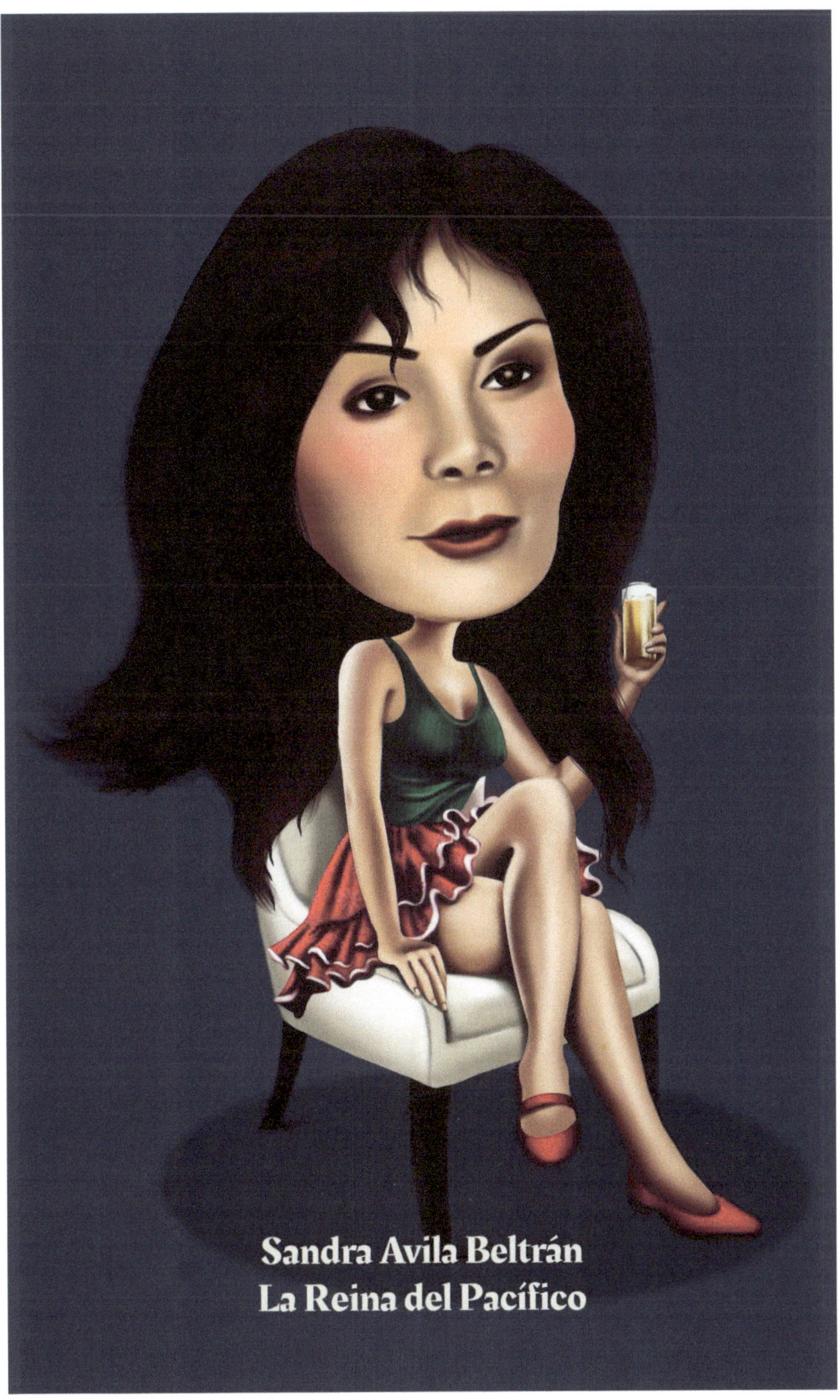

Sandra Avila Beltrán
La Reina del Pacífico

soon after.

Like Griselda Blanco, Beltrán is capable of extreme violence although she appears to be much more circumspect in her actions. Unlike Blanco who was not what you'd call a great beauty, Beltrán is very attractive, maybe even sexy, and a home grown Mexican legend. She is the subject of popular songs and even the inspiration for a Mexican soap opera series, *La Reina del Sur*. Her looks are an asset that she carefully protects with plastic surgery and a fondness for always having her makeup just right. In 2011 while in prison she somehow managed to have a doctor give her Botox injections resulting in two prison officials being fired.

Beltrán had numerous affairs with various drug kingpins either for convenience or to strategically position herself with as many useful contacts as possible. She was married twice, both times to corrupt ex-police commanders who decided the drug business paid better than policing. Both ended up being killed. Beltrán's last known beau is Juan Diego Espinoza Ramirez, *The Tiger*, a bigwig in the Colombian Norte del Valle Cartel, further strengthening the Borgia-like alliance between the Mexican and Colombian drug cartels.

Beltrán's particular expertise was in money laundering but she eventually got in trouble when police were able to connect her and Ramirez to nine tons of cocaine on board a ship in the Port of Manzanillo, Colima in 2001. She and Ramirez managed to avoid arrest until 2007 when she was convicted of money laundering billions of dollars' worth of drugs smuggled from Colombia to Mexico. Charges were dropped in 2011 but then she was extradited to the U.S. in 2012 on drug possession and trafficking charges. After making a plea deal admitting only to providing financial assistance to Ramirez, she was deported back to Mexico where she was promptly rearrested and convicted on money laundering charges. Her sentence was ultimately revoked by a Mexican judge based on the fact she had already been tried for the same crime in the United States. As she left jail, she was picked up by a convoy of luxury SUVs, unlike common criminals who are sent packing with little more than the shirt on their backs.

Beltrán's good looks, expensive life style, and expertise in the finer points of money laundering all add up to a larger than life character, a woman who even when arrested would reportedly not appear before the press without first making sure her makeup was just right.

Claudia Ochoa Felix
The Empress of Antrax

You would think one prima donna for the distaff organized crime world would be enough but like Pop Star divas all vying for the female version of the John Gotti Award, there's competition. If Sandra Avila Beltrán thought, she was the 'fairest of them all' she better look hard into her magic mirror. Like most areas of life, youth and beauty ultimately wins out. Her rival for queen of drugs and bloodshed is the twenty-seven-year-old beauty, Claudia Ochoa Felix, a woman with killer looks and social media skills to match.

Beltrán may be the *La Reina del Pacífico, Queen of the Pacific*, but her rival Ochoa Felix, is *Empress of Antrax*. If the nickname didn't give it away already, *Los Antrax*, is the deadly security arm and kill-squad of the Sinaloa Cartel named after the deadly disease anthrax. The Sinaloa Cartel is considered by U.S. intelligence to be the largest drug cartel in the world, responsible for the vast majority of heroin that enters the United States.

Ochoa Felix is not your Meyer Lansky type, carefully keeping a low profile, working in the shadows; no, not this Mexican Kim Kardashian want-to-be. She consistently posts sexy pictures of herself, posing butt or breast first, in skin-tight mini dresses or lounging seductively in skimpy bikinis, often holding her favorite custom painted pink graffiti-inspired AK-47. This self-promoting *sicario* of bad taste has over thirty-five thousand followers on Twitter and Instagram. I'm not sure if this says more about her colossal ego or the public's insatiable appetite for bad girl celebrities. No matter what the public thinks, the lady has game, and her talents extend beyond her larger-than-life breasts and buttock. With the arrests of the two male leaders of *Los Antrax*, one of whom was Claudia's old lover, word is our girl is the new boss.

Claudia originally kept a low profile, until twenty-three-year old look-alike, Yurina Castillo Torres, was mistakenly assassinated. Now she uses social media like a public relations professional posting lavish lifestyle and party photos seemly unconcerned about her high profile image. Bodyguards always surround her but that's no guarantee of longevity. Since 2006, the deadly Mexican drug wars have claimed an estimated one hundred thousand lives.

Melissa Margarita Calderon Ojeda
La China

The arrest of Melissa Margarita Calderon Ojeda, *La China*, a leading cartel assassin, on information provided by her lover and second-in-command, Hector Pedro Camarena Gomez, also known as *El Chino*,

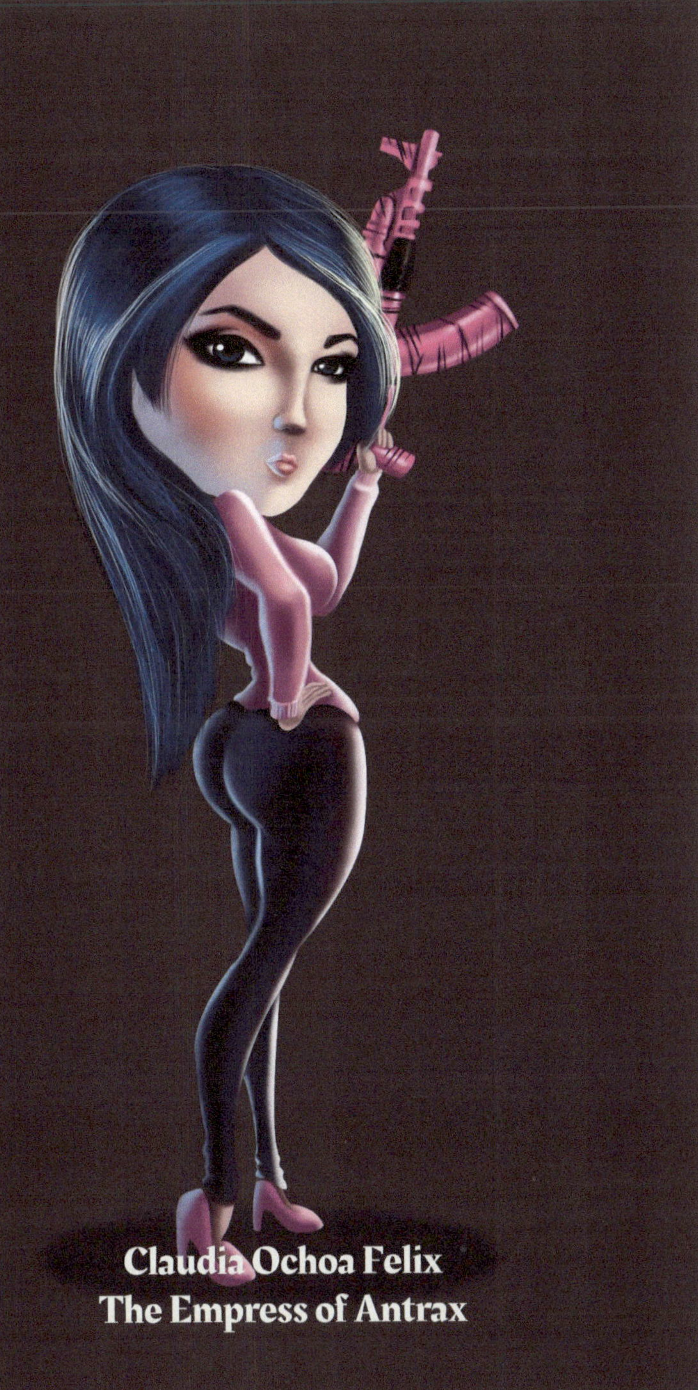

**Claudia Ochoa Felix
The Empress of Antrax**

in order to get a lighter sentence after his arrest only proves that love, loyalty, and libidinous liaisons amongst gangsters is a liability. El Chino was kind enough to take the authorities to a mass grave where his paramour dumped her victims, at least those that she didn't dispose of by leaving them on the doorstep of grieving relatives. Calderon Ojeda is believed to be responsible for approximately one hundred and fifty murders over a ten-year period, and she is expected to be directly responsible for nine murders herself. Calderon Ojeda managed to survive in the male dominated Mexican crime organization by being as nasty and violent as her male counterparts.

Thirty-year old Calderon Ojeda was arrested at the Los Cabos Airport without incident. Her life of crime began in 2005 when she dated a member of the Damaso Cartel. She rose quickly through the ranks. The Damaso Cartel is associated with the Sinaloa Cartel, an organization regarded by US intelligence as the most powerful drug cartel in the world.

Despite her reputation for violence and mayhem that rivalled her male colleagues, the macho Mexican crime organization decided to demote Calderon Ojeda after the release from prison of one of its previous leaders; they obviously are not an advocate of women's lib. The corporate slight caused her to form her own little entrepreneurial band of gangsters.

Beauty and The Bust

Ochoa Felix and Beltrán might be the main rivals for the queen of crime, but no discussion of drugs, beauty, and craziness would be complete without a list of honourable-mentions. The article "The 10

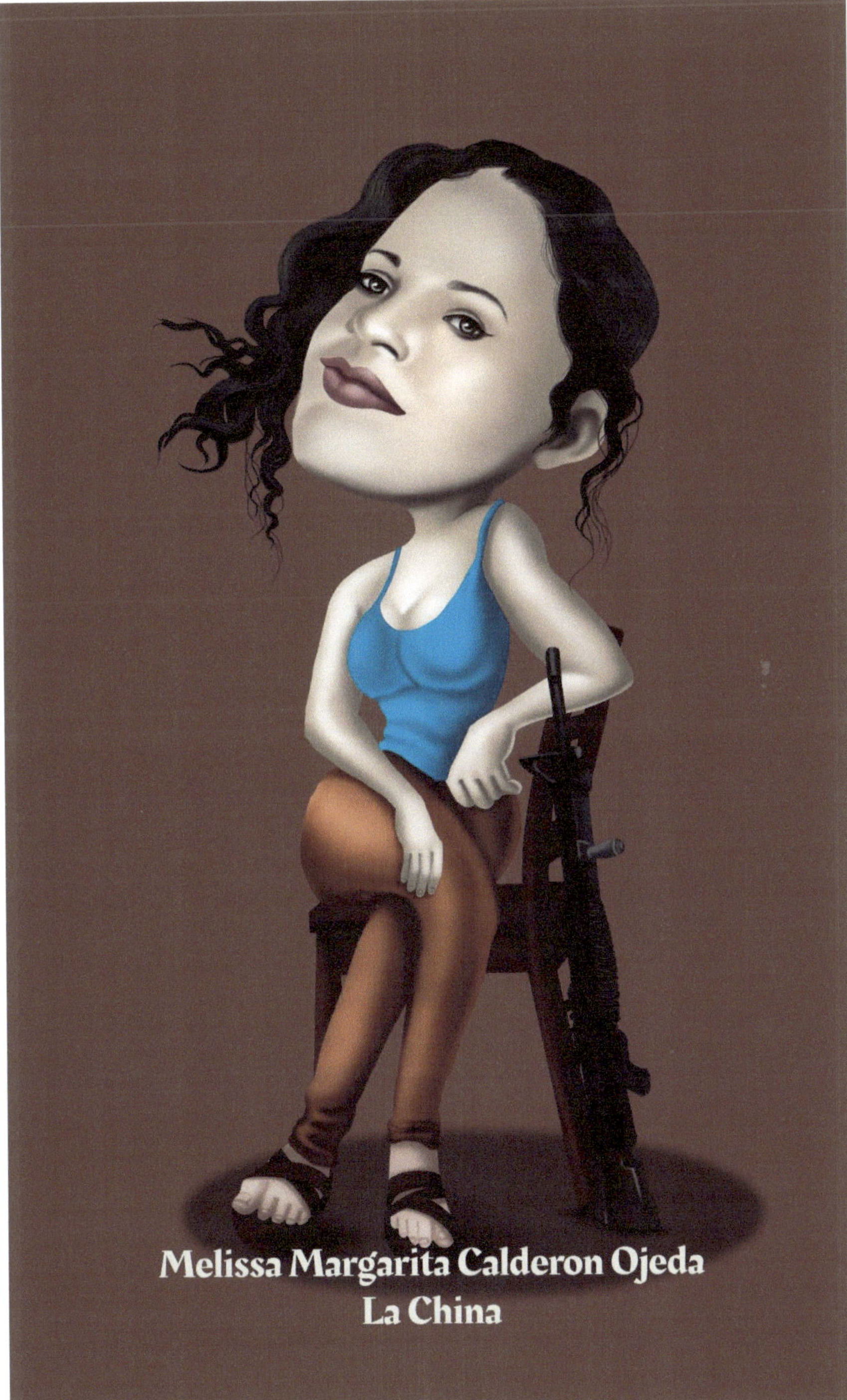

Melissa Margarita Calderon Ojeda
La China

Sexiest Drug Smugglers And Traffickers" found on thefix.com website has as good a list as any. Despite their beauty and talent, they all ended up being busted and spending time in jail. None of the following women ever reached the extremes of commercial success or societal depravity as Ochoa Felix or Beltrán, but who can resist a badass beauty with self-destructive tendencies?

Martha Heredia
Latin American Idol

We start with Martha Heredia, winner of the 2009 *Latin American Idol*. Unfortunately winning a television-singing contest is no guarantee of success. It didn't help her career when in 2010 she accidently killed a pedestrian in a car accident. Of course as soon as your singing career goes into the dumper, the obvious next step is drug trafficking. In 2013 our songbird beauty was arrested on a flight from the Dominican Republic to New York for trying to smuggle 2.9 pounds of heroin in the heels of three platform shoes. I always wondered why anyone would wear platform shoes, now I know, but why three, don't shoes usually come in pairs?

Domino Harvey
Bounty Hunter

Domino Harvey can't really be classified as an organized crime figure, if truth be told she is just another rich kid gone bad, but when beauty and privilege turns into a tragic pursuit of adrenaline and drug related highs, then perhaps, it is a story worth telling. Domino Harvey is not the only daughter of well-known celebrities whose life spiralled out of control, but she is probably the only one that went from fashion model to lesbian drug-addicted bounty

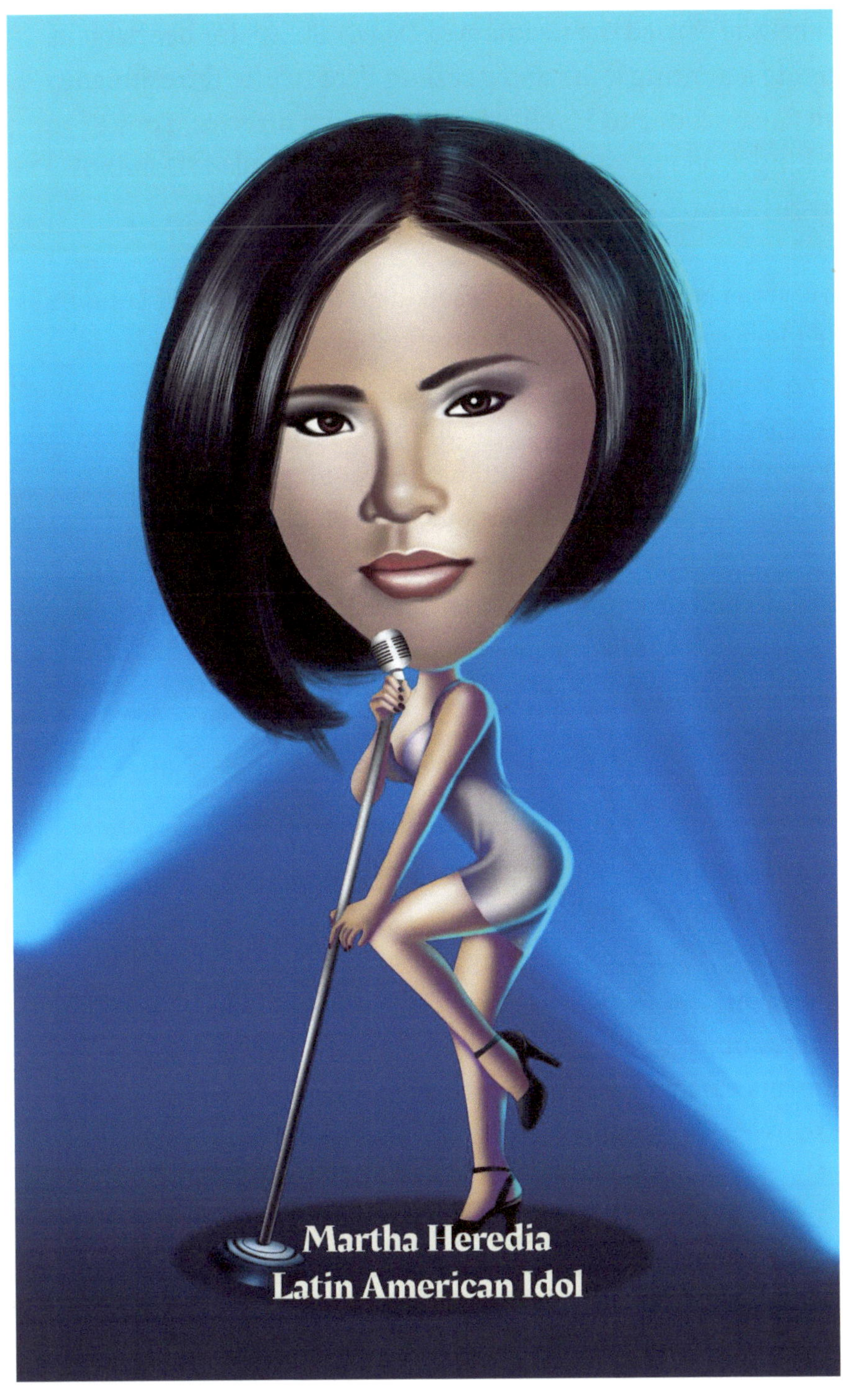
Martha Heredia
Latin American Idol

hunter. She earned the nicknamed *Dagger Baileys* for her habit of carrying a hunting knife and guzzling her favorite refreshment, Irish Cream Liqueur. Her life fascinated film director, Tony Scott, resulting in a long association and a 2005 film called "Domino" starring Keira Knightley.

Harvey was born in 1969 and raised in an upscale area of London called Belgravia. Her father was well-respected actor Laurence Harvey who appeared in many movies throughout the 1950s and 60s. He earned an Oscar nomination for his role in *Room at the Top* (1959). Her mother was Vogue fashion model Pauline Stone. Her father died in 1973 when she was just four years old. As a child Domino was a tomboy more inclined to play with toy soldiers and action figures than dolls and princess costumes. She learned martial arts and practised what she learned on the local boys. She attended a series of fancy boarding schools frequently getting expelled from many of them.

As she grew into a teenager her good looks and most likely her mother's connections managed to get her work as a model with the prestigious Ford Modelling Agency, but she hated the work, preferring grittier forms of employment. She studied sound engineering and worked as a DJ in the London Clubs. She even managed one of them for a while. Eventually she moved to Southern California catching up to her mother who had moved there when she married American entrepreneur Peter Morton, co-founder of the Hard Rock Café.

After a series of jobs she trained as an EMT and applied for work at the Los Angeles Fire Department but was rejected. She then enrolled in a course to become a bail recovery agent, a bounty hunter, and

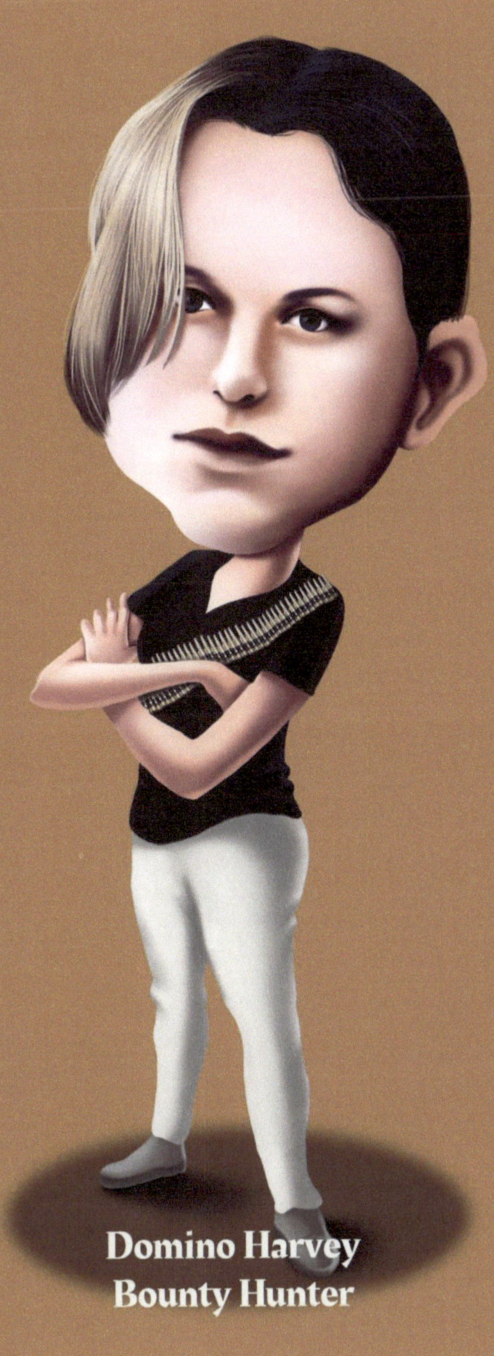

Domino Harvey
Bounty Hunter

yes, you can go to school to learn to be a thug. After graduating she worked with her teacher Ed Martinez at a bail bonds operation also run by Celes King III, an interesting fellow who went from civil rights leader to real estate broker to bail bondsman. I'm not sure which profession is sleazier, real estate or bounty hunting, in any case, the work was just the kind of thing to appeal to Harvey's deepening bizarre attraction to guns, violence, and drugs. Her hobbies were not what you'd expect from your average five foot nine inch ex fashion model: collecting knives, swords, and AK-47s. She spent three years pursuing drug dealers, thieves, and the occasional murderer. It was her kind of life style, wild and dangerous.

Harvey didn't make much money as a bounty hunter but that didn't seem to bother her. She lived above the garage of her mother's Beverly Hills home. She loved the work but the job, life style, and criminal associations, led her to drugs. The bounty hunters would often keep whatever drugs they found after capturing one of their targets. She spent time in drug rehab clinics on four separate occasions all paid for by her mother. On one occasion she rehabbed in Hawaii but on her return she was unable to get her old job back.

In 2003 she was arrested for possession of crystal meth. She pleaded guilty and tried rehab one more time. She was arrested again in 2005 on charges of trafficking methamphetamines but she denied the charges. After three weeks in jail she was placed under house arrest and ordered to wear an ankle monitor. She hired someone to live with her to make sure she did not relapse but on June 27, 2005 she was found unconscious in the bathtub. She was taken to the hospital but never regained consciousness. She died from an overdose of the painkiller fentanyl that mimics the effects of heroine.

For most of the women discussed, crime is a business: Al Pacino's character, Michael Corleone, describes it perfectly in *The Godfather*, "It's not personal Sonny, it's strictly business;" perhaps that's the difference between people like Domino Harvey and Gertrude Lythgoe.

Lisette Lee
The Pot Princess of Beverly Hills

Lisette Lee also dubbed, *The Korean Paris Hilton*, don't ask me why, claimed to be a Samsung Corporation heiress, but like most of her claims it's utter nonsense. Lee left South Korea as a young girl and headed for the bright lights of Beverly Hills where she adopted a variety of personalities. She eventually hooked up with a low-level drug-dealer, David Garrett. Together they put together a crew and proceeded to move large quantities of marijuana from Los Angeles to Columbus, Ohio. One has to wonder what these two geniuses were thinking when they were arrested at the Port Columbus International Airport by DEA agents when they landed from Van Nuys, California with thirteen large suitcases, two assistants, a body guard, and five hundred pounds of marijuana. Bravado and bullshit might have been her stock and trade but ultimately she admitted to the authorities of moving almost seven thousand pounds of marijuana from LA to Columbus.

Chatchaya Cuesta Ramos
aka Yuyee

There really isn't a whole lot you can say about a beautiful ex model and television actress who is about to spend the next fifteen years in jail for trying to smuggle 251 milligrams of cocaine in a chocolate

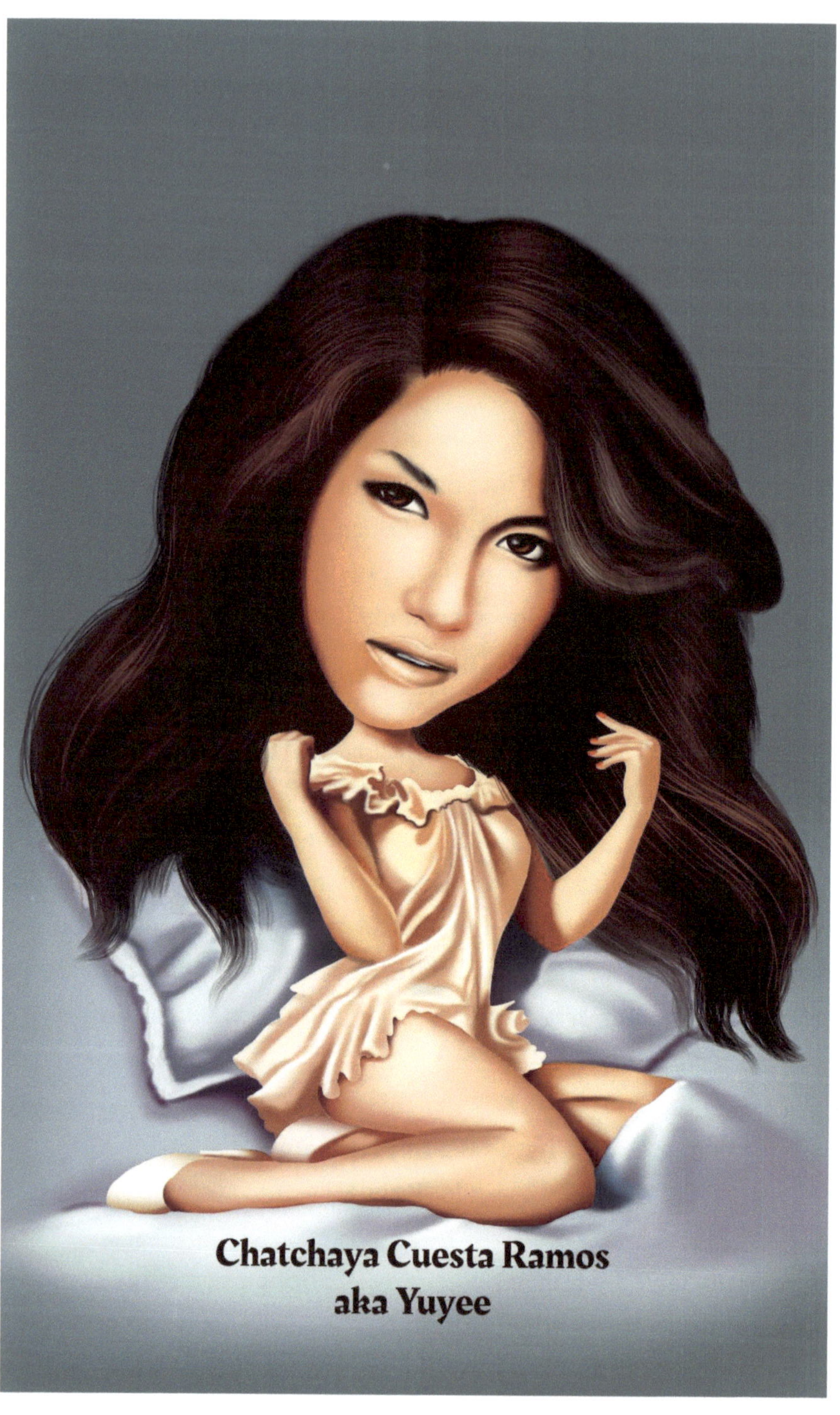

Chatchaya Cuesta Ramos
aka Yuyee

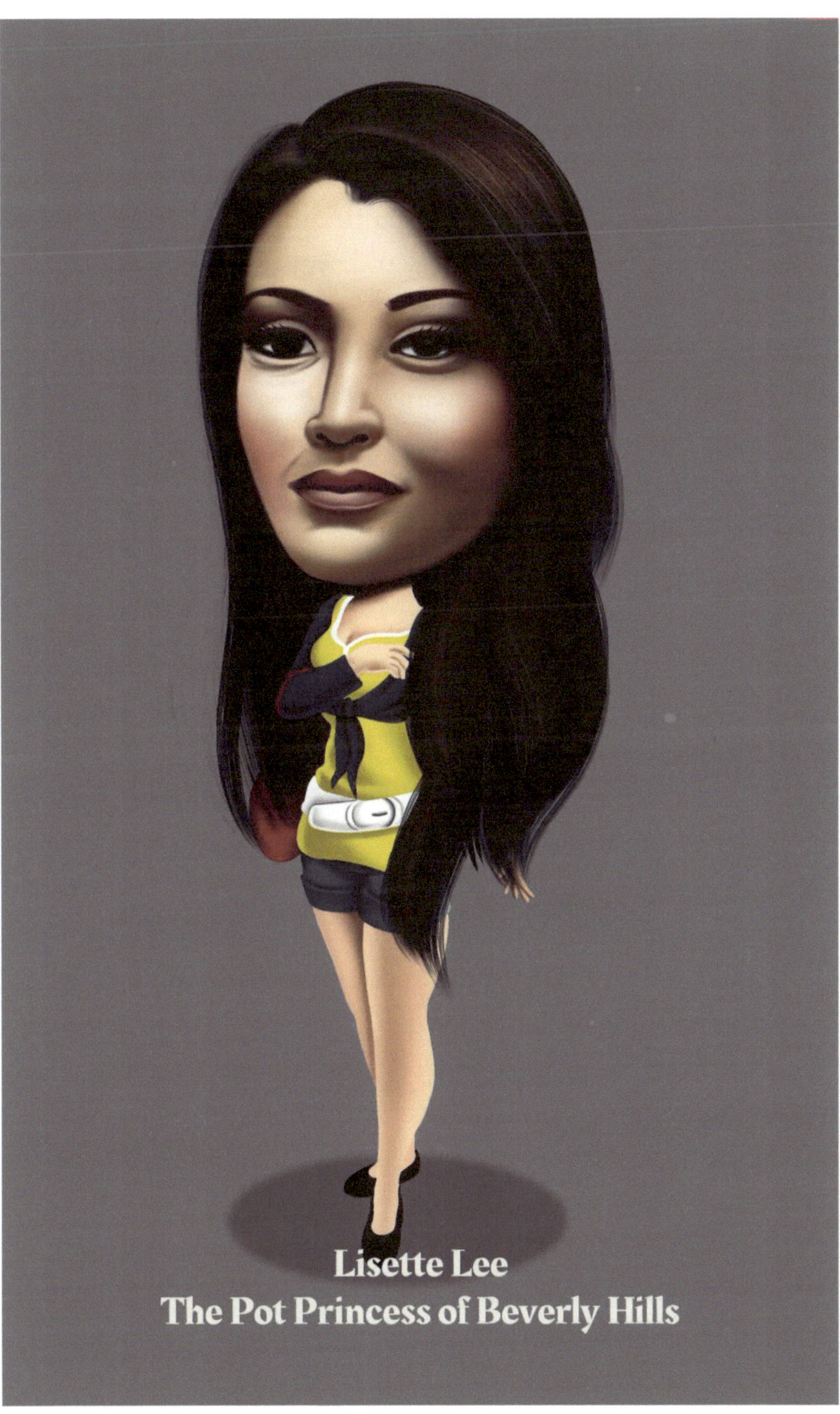

Lisette Lee
The Pot Princess of Beverly Hills

package into Thailand from Vietnam. Ramos claimed the drugs were for her personal use but the judge wasn't buying it. I guess he didn't like her television show. To add insult to injury, an additional three months were tacked on when authorities searched her home and found she was illegally keeping exotic animals including, an Asian Golden Cat, three rare turtles, and over twenty snakes.

She claimed she was just taking care of the exotic creatures until she could release them into the wild. Granted her exploits are not in the same class as most of these other women, but her good looks help her make the list.

Samantha Scarlino

Samantha Scarlino, a Miss Italia finalist in 1999, is one of the modelling beauty queens who found the jet set life somehow lacking. Her pursuit of a higher-octane lifestyle must have been fuelled by a desire for more money, a bigger adrenalin rush, or perhaps just a self-indulgent need for the next cocaine high.

Her high-flying modelling career provided the perfect cover for a while, but like most criminals, the good times eventually caught up to her. Scarlino along with twenty-two other people were arrested for their involvement in a major drug ring. Police found eleven hundred pounds of cocaine in a hotel in Milan. Scarlino was accused of transporting cash from Italy to Peru intended for the drug cartels.

Authorities also linked the Italian beauty with the two women dubbed the "Peru 2." Melissa Reid and Michaela McCollum were arrested in Lima Peru for trying to smuggle two and half million dollars-worth of cocaine into South America.

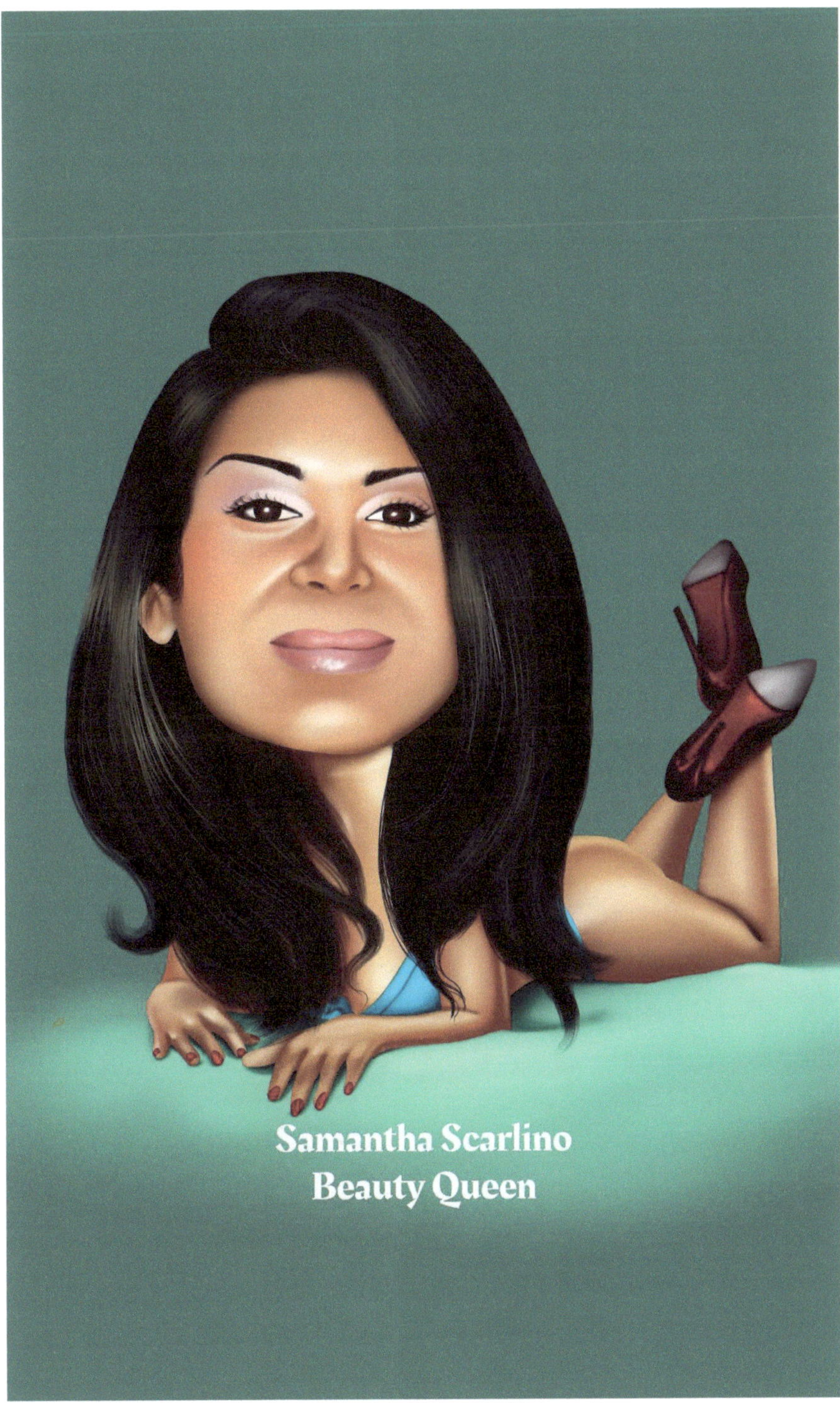

Samantha Scarlino
Beauty Queen

Simone Farrow
The Ice Queen

Simone Farrow, also known as Simone Cheung, and Simone Starr, is another of the gorgeous models who found posing for Penthouse and modelling Ed Hardy swimsuits just wasn't enough of a kick, so she decided that dealing "ice" was a nice little income supplement, especially since she was already a habitual abuser. Ice also referred to as shabu or crystal is the purest form of methamphetamine. It comes in powder or crystals so it can be snorted, injected, or smoked, kind of a death wish of your choice. Farrow smuggled the ice into Australia hidden in bath salts earning a hefty return bloating her bank balance.

Farrow blames her promiscuous, drug addicted mother for her poor life choices. She told an Australian court that her mother locked her in her room, and even took her to a brothel when she was seventeen telling her it was okay to be a prostitute. While working as an escort she claims her pimp held her upside down over the edge of an apartment in Sydney, something he must have seen in a Jason Stratham movie. Farrow's poor up bringing wasn't helped by her battle with a bipolar condition, depression, and her dependency on Xanax, a habit her psychiatrist said caused her to lapse into periods of unconsciousness.

Farrow was arrested in 2012 and pleaded guilty the following year to "importing a marketable quantity of a border controlled drug." She was accused of being the ringleader of an international drug ring but she denied being the boss, claiming she was setup by her colleagues who managed to get control of her bank, phone, and email accounts. She claimed they even passed themselves off as her

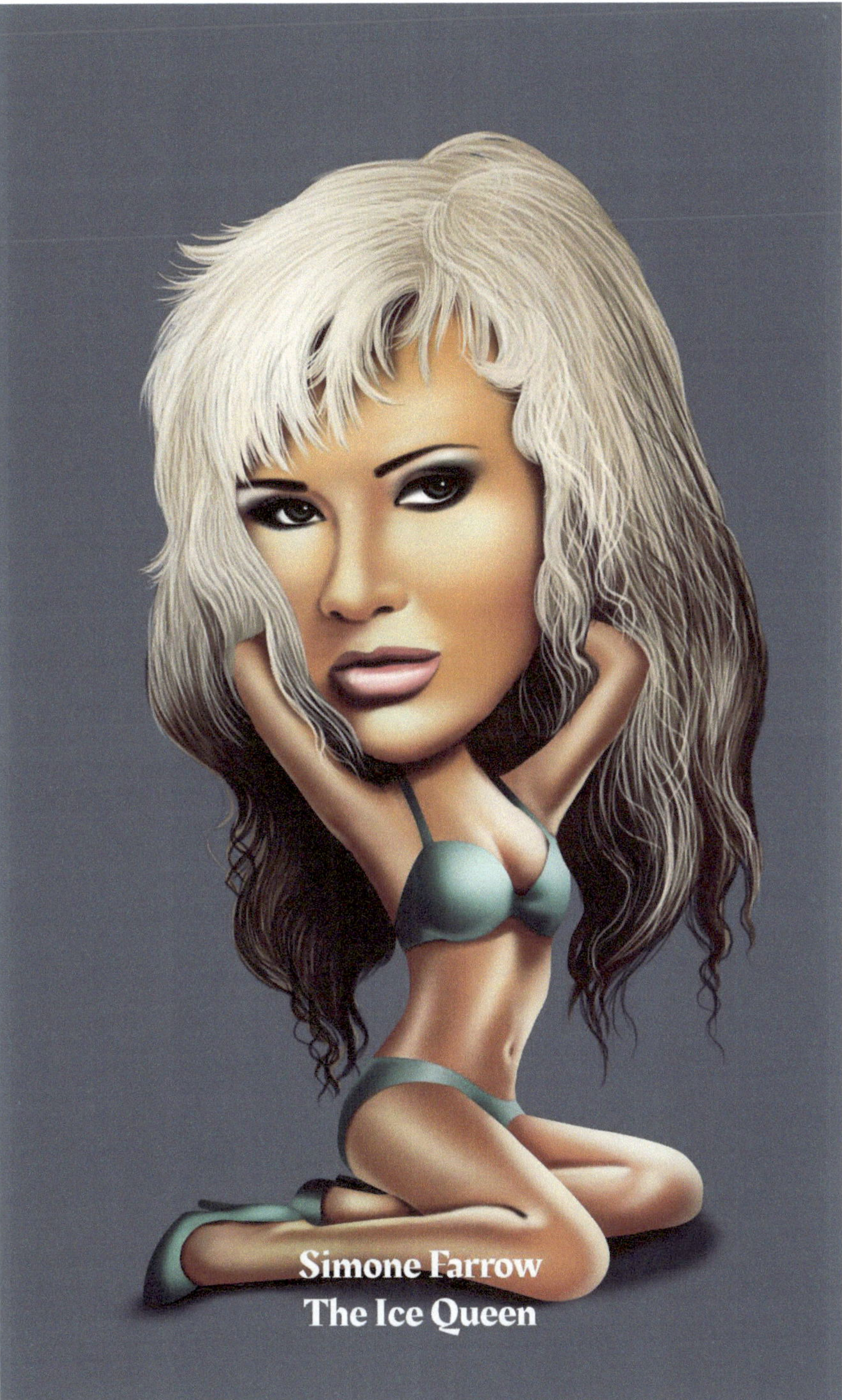
Simone Farrow
The Ice Queen

by imitating her voice: however, witnesses in court claimed they dealt directly with Farrow paying her seven thousand dollars an ounce.

Angie Sanselmente Valencia
Coffee Queen

A career in crime seemed inevitable for this South American beauty that couldn't even play it straight for a beauty pageant. In 2000 she won the prestigious *Reinado Internacional del Café, the International Queen of Coffee*, title but was disqualified two days later because she was married. Her next gig was as a lingerie model, ultimately graduating to international drug peddler.

She was arrested in Buenos Aires, Argentina in 2010 after one of her drug mule angels, a twenty-one-year-old beauty, "Ariel L", was arrested with a suitcase containing 121 pounds of cocaine. No attempt was made to hide the drugs leading authorities to conclude "Ariel L" had help from airport employees. The investigation eventually led to Valencia's arrest and conviction.

She blamed her conviction for drug trafficking on the fact that she is a Colombian. Prejudice or not, she was sentenced to six years and eight months in jail for supposedly operating one of the world's largest drug operations using a cadre of beautiful woman paid five thousand dollars each to smuggle cocaine into England from Argentina through Mexico. Her claim of innocence was somewhat tainted by her former association with ex-boyfriend, the Mexican drug boss known by the quaint moniker *The Monster*. After serving half her sentence she was deported from Argentina back to Colombia.

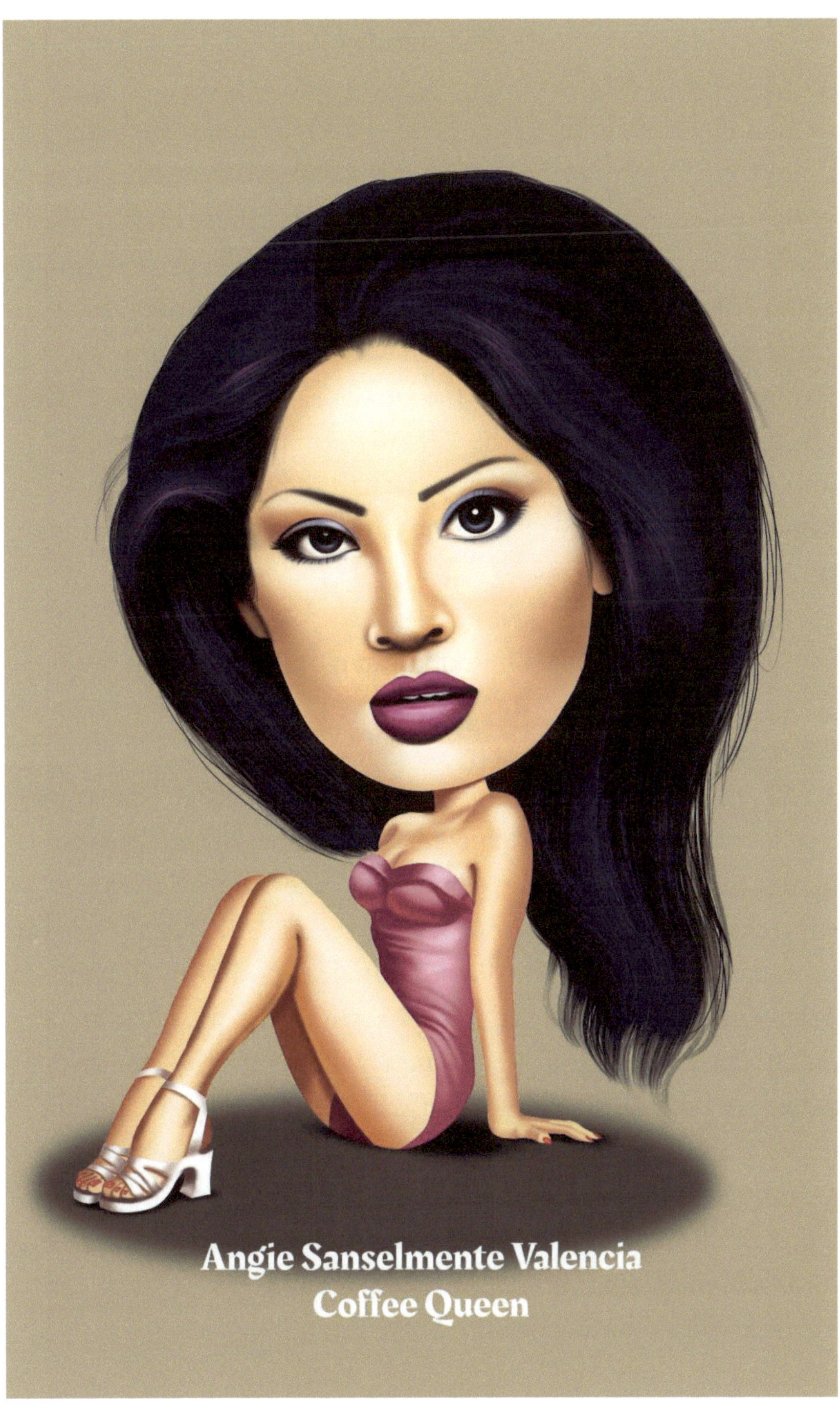

Angie Sanselmente Valencia
Coffee Queen

Krista Boseley

Canadian Playboy model Krista Boseley and her colleague Gilles Joseph Pierre Lapointe were arrested at Orange County's John Wayne Airport on charges of conspiracy to distribute ecstasy after Homeland Security agents with the aid of Kirby, the drug-sniffing German Sheppard, found 40 kilograms of MDMA powder and 50,000 ecstasy pills. Part of the stash was found in Lapointe's carry on, while the rest was found on the small private plane they arrived on. In addition to the drugs the Canadian pair also carried large amounts of US currency that they insisted they had won at the Bellagio in Los Vegas. Boseley denied any knowledge of the drugs Lapointe was transporting.

Anna Chapman
The Red Under The Bed

Anna Chapman is a different bird of prey. This Russian beauty was a secret agent arrested and convicted as a member of the Illegal's Program run by the Russian Federation's external intelligence agency, the SVR (Sluzhba Vneshney Razvedki). The Illegals Program planted sleeper agents in the West in order to gather intelligence for Russia's equivalent of the CIA, the SVR. Chapman wasn't your standard Cold War, nondescript, mousy, fade-into-the-woodwork so you don't draw attention to yourself kind of spy, no *siree*. This hot chick was, and probably still is, a party animal that when living in New York liked to eat in the best restaurants and hangout at the trendiest clubs. This made-for-TV Russian bombshell appeared in the Russian magazine version of *Maxim* complete with black negligee and automatic pistol.

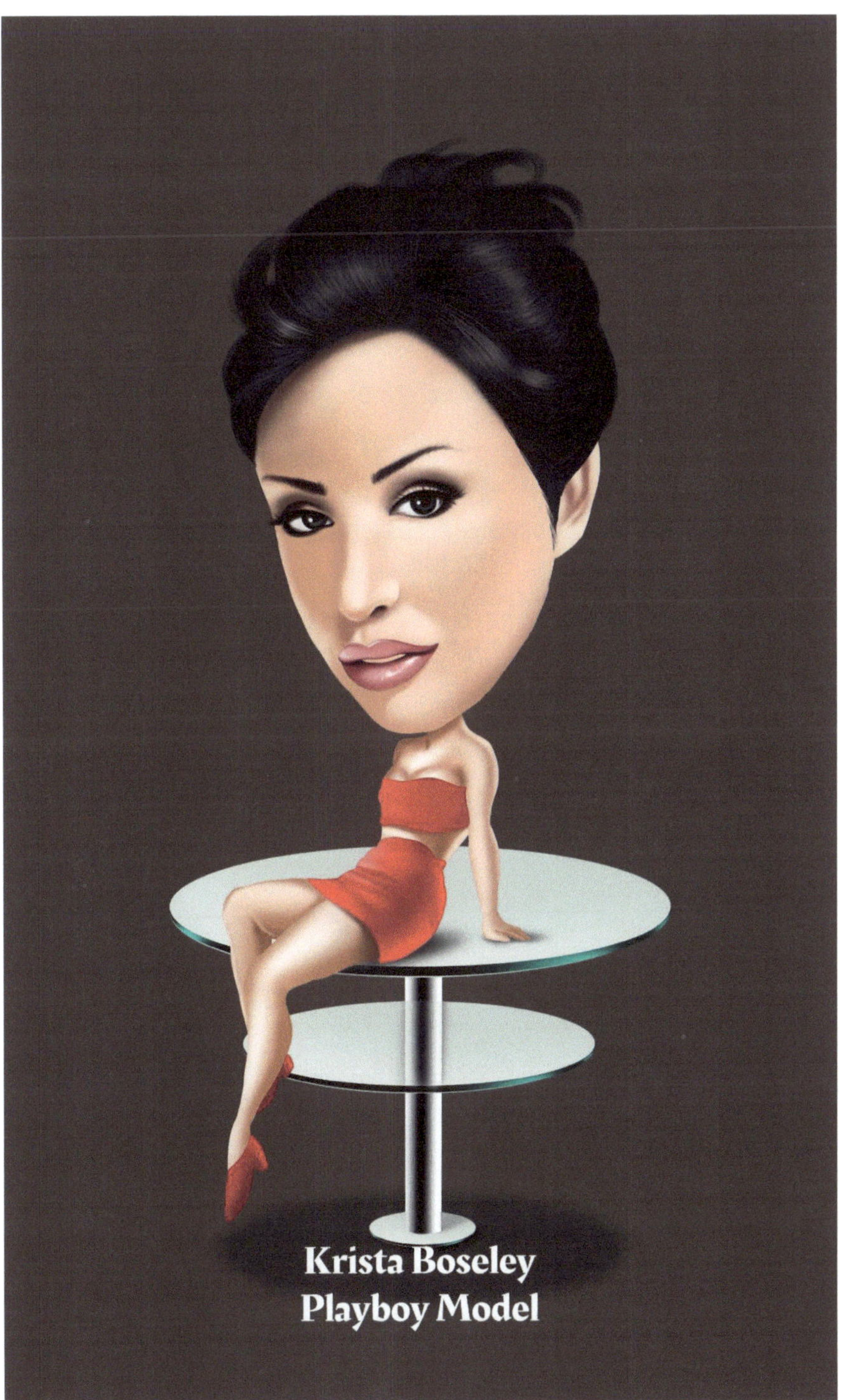

Krista Boseley
Playboy Model

Chapman was born Anna Vasil'yevna Kushchenko in 1982 in Volgograd to Vasily Kushchenko, a senior KGB official (now the SVR). Papa officially holds a senior position at the MID (Foreign Affairs Department). Chapman's ex-husband, British psychologist Alex Chapman, told MI5 that when he and Anna visited her father in Zimbabwe, he appeared to be scary, secretive, and surrounded by a lot more security than other diplomats.

Anna isn't just some sexy bimbo; she's a sexy bimbo with brains and a Master's degree in economics. She moved to London in the early 2000s where she met Chapman at a rave party. Her marriage to Chapman allowed her to obtain a British passport while retaining her Russian citizenship. In Britain she held well-paying jobs at Barclay's Bank and Navigator Asset Management. She divorced Chapman in 2006 and returned to Russia before moving to New York in 2007 where she established an online international real estate company called PropertyFinder LLC. According to Alex Chapman she told him the company was continually short of funds and in debt, but in 2009 she suddenly had enough backing to employee fifty people.

The FBI had been keeping an eye on Chapman and her network, under their Operation Ghost Stories sting. By 2010 she was under arrest along with ten other Russian sleeper agents, one of whom was working for Microsoft. Another spy was caught in Cyprus but two others managed to escape. Chapman was accused of coming to the U.S. to gather intelligence for the SVR. She was caught after she accepted a fake passport from an FBI agent with instructions to pass it on to another spy. After speaking to her father who advised her that it was a trap, she turned the passport over to the local police. She was arrested anyway along with her fellow secret agents.

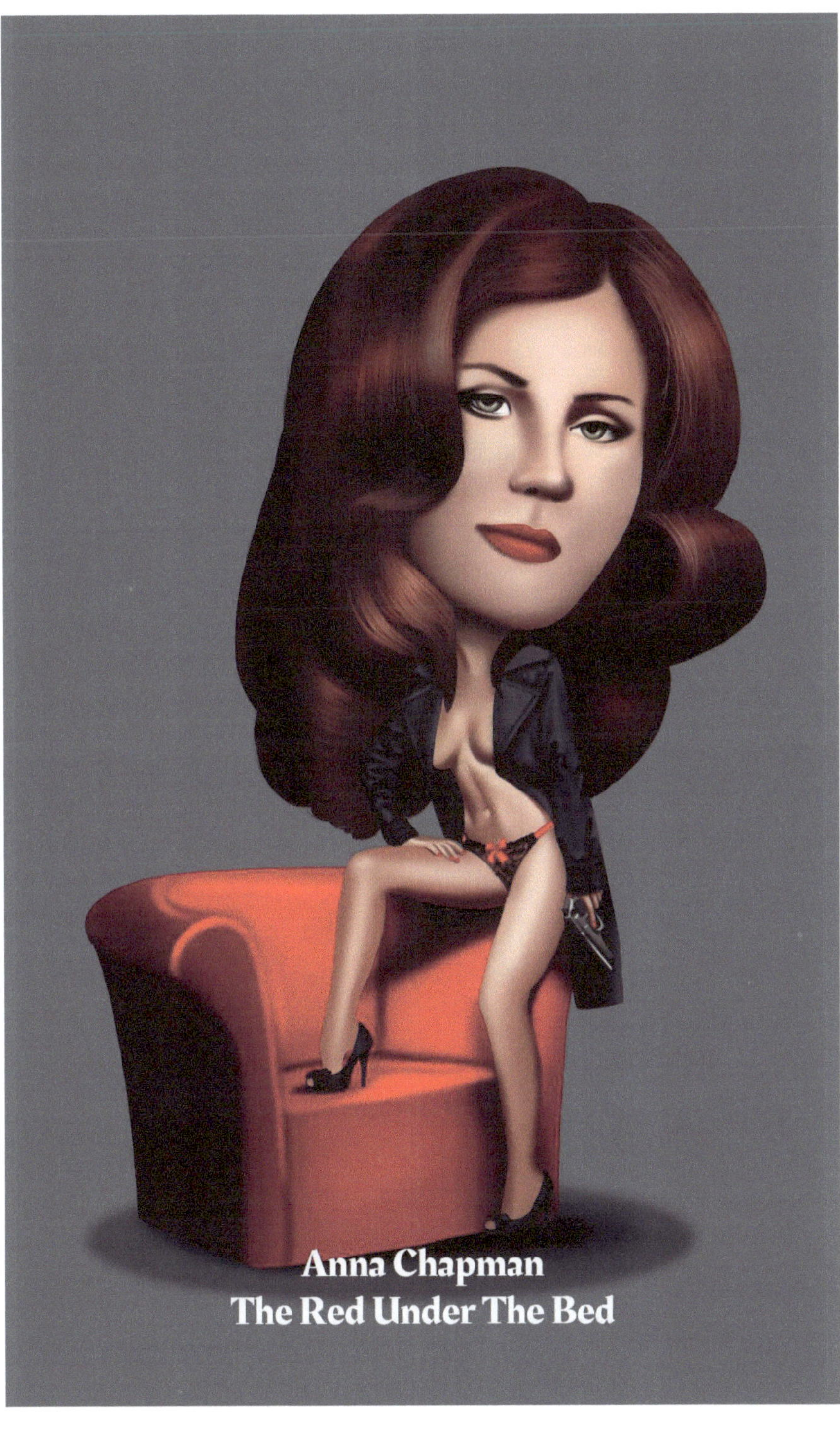

Anna Chapman
The Red Under The Bed

Later it was revealed that her arrest was most likely prompted by a plan she was hatching to seduce a high-ranking member of President Obama's cabinet in a 'honeytrap.' She pleaded guilty to a charge of conspiracy to act as an agent of a foreign government without notifying the U.S. Attorney General. She was deported in a prisoner exchange swap with the Russians. Back in Moscow she testified in the trial of Colonel Alexander Poteyev (*in absentia*) that her arrest was prompted when Poteyev provided the FBI with information, and a secret code used by the American agent who contacted her, that only Poteyev and her handler knew.

When she arrived in Russia she promptly appeared in Russia's version of *Maxim* magazine posing seductively wearing a see-through black negligee while holding an automatic pistol. The magazine listed her as one of Russia's 100 sexiest women. Nobody could accuse her of being a one trick pony: in addition to her spying and modelling careers, she was also employed as an investment adviser to the President of the Fundservice Bank, a Moscow bank that handles government payouts to private aerospace businesses.

She also hosts her own weekly television show, *Secrets of the World* on REN TV, and she's an editor for *Venture Business News*. If that wasn't enough she also was involved in a foundation that supported the second International Conference on 'The Genetics of Aging and Longevity." All-in-all Anna Chapman is a busy girl.

Chapman wanted to return to the United Kingdom but the British government revoked her citizenship and barred her re-entry using the rarely used, National Immigration and Asylum Act of 2002, and the Immigration Asylum and Nationality Act of 2006.

Rosetta Cutolo
Ice Eyes

Unlike some of the beautiful women who tried to extend their jet set beauty queen lifestyles by supplementing their incomes with drug trafficking, Rosetta Cutolo, born 1937, aka *Ice Eyes* (*Occh'egghiaccio*) is the real mafia deal. Her younger brother, Raffaele Cutolo, born 1941, is head of the Camorra crime syndicate, Nuova Camorra Organizzata (NCO). The Camorra originated in the region of Campania with Naples as its capital. Unlike the more disciplined Sicilian Mafia with its top-down hierarchy and strict code of conduct, the Camorra is more horizontal in structure with independent crews constantly feuding.

Since Raffaele has spent most of his life in jail, the day-to-day operations of the NCO fell to his older sister, known for her able negotiating skills when dealing with the Sicilian and South African cocaine dealers. Raffaele continued to provide leadership from his prison cell with Rosetta carrying out his grand plans.

Raffaele was prone to seek attention by giving interviews and making speeches in the courtroom, something that infuriated his sister, often leading to heated arguments. Rosetta preferred to stay out of the spotlight ruling the family crime business from her 365-room sixteenth century headquarters, the Castle Mediceo, a multi-billion lire estate complete with a large park, tennis courts, and a swimming pool. Perhaps that's not exactly keeping a low profile but at least she avoided grandstanding like her brother.

Negotiating drug deals with the South Africans wasn't her only talent; she didn't shy away from the more violent aspects of her mandate. She even attempted to blow-up a local police headquarters. This was no small-time beauty queen operation; under Rosetta's guidance the NCO was deeply involved in the garbage, dairy, fish, and coffee businesses, even politics. She ran the NCO for fifteen years and became one of the most powerful criminal figures in organized crime.

Rosetta spent twelve years on the run after a 1981 police raid on her headquarters. She managed to get smuggled out of the grounds by hiding under a rug in a car driven by a neighbourhood priest. She managed to continue guiding operations from a series of safe houses. Eventually in 1993, she was arrested and convicted of various Mafia related charges, but she did manage to avoid being convicted on nine counts of murder. She was sentenced to nine years in jail but the sentence was later reduced to five. Whether the light sentence was a matter of corruption and contacts or lack of reliable evidence due to her low profile approach remains a matter of speculation.

<h3 align="center">Raffaella D'Alterio
Miciona, The Big Female Kitten</h3>

Unlike the highly organized Sicilian Mafia that structures itself in a business-like hierarchical manner, the Camorra Mafia resists such structural discipline and prefers to operate more like feuding medieval warlords but with access to deadly weapons and modern technologies.

Rosetta Cutolo's husband Raffaele made attempts to reorganize the Camorra under the banner of the New Organized Camorra (Nuova

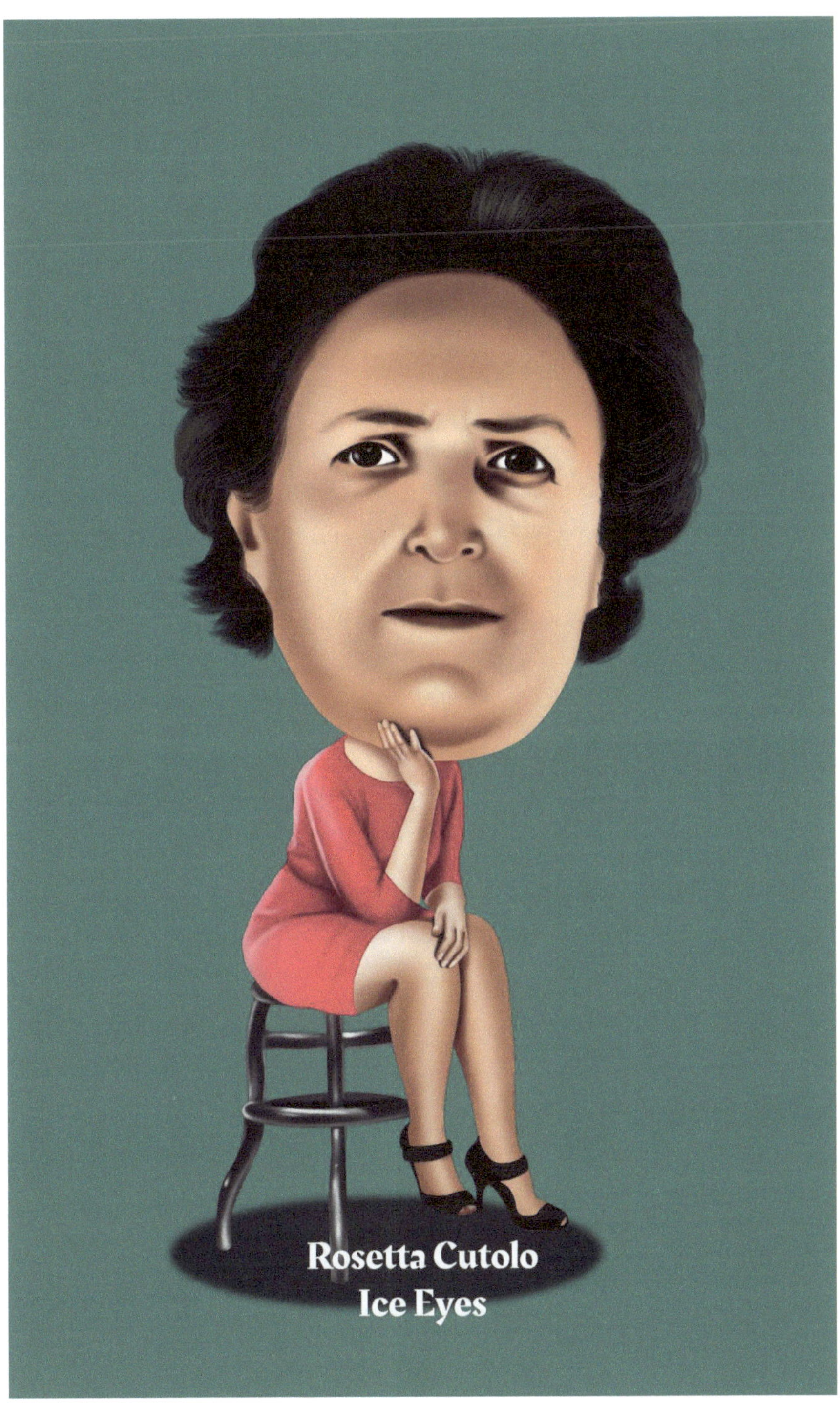

Rosetta Cutolo
Ice Eyes

Camorra Organizzata or NCO) under his leadership, but clan infighting, jealousy, and greed came more naturally to the one hundred and eleven Camorra clans encompassing over sixty-seven hundred members in and around the southern port city of Naples. Authorities estimate the Camorra generates an estimated two hundred and eighteen billion dollars a year.

The warfare between clans was highlighted by numerous drive-by shootings resulting in civilian, as well as, Mafioso casualties. The Scampia Feud in 2004 and 2005 between the Di Lauro clan and the Scissionisti resulted in over one hundred street-killings. In 2006 another war broke out with twenty different Camorra clans involved at the cost of twelve lives in ten days. Over the last thirty years it is estimated that these warring factions have killed more than four thousand people.

One of those that died in 2006 was Nicola Pianese whose wife Raffaella D'Alterio took over and ran the clan earning the nickname, *Miciona*, or *The Big Female Kitten*, but this kitten had claws and she wasn't afraid to use them; nor were her rivals who attempted to kill her three years into her reign as queen of the Pianese-D'Alterio Camorrra Clan. D'Alterio's operation included extortion, counterfeiting, drug trafficking, waste disposal, and construction.

In 2012 D'Alterio and sixty-five members of her clan were arrested in a police operation that also seized twenty million dollars-worth of cars and property. Raffaella D'Alterio definitely makes any list of organized crime queens.

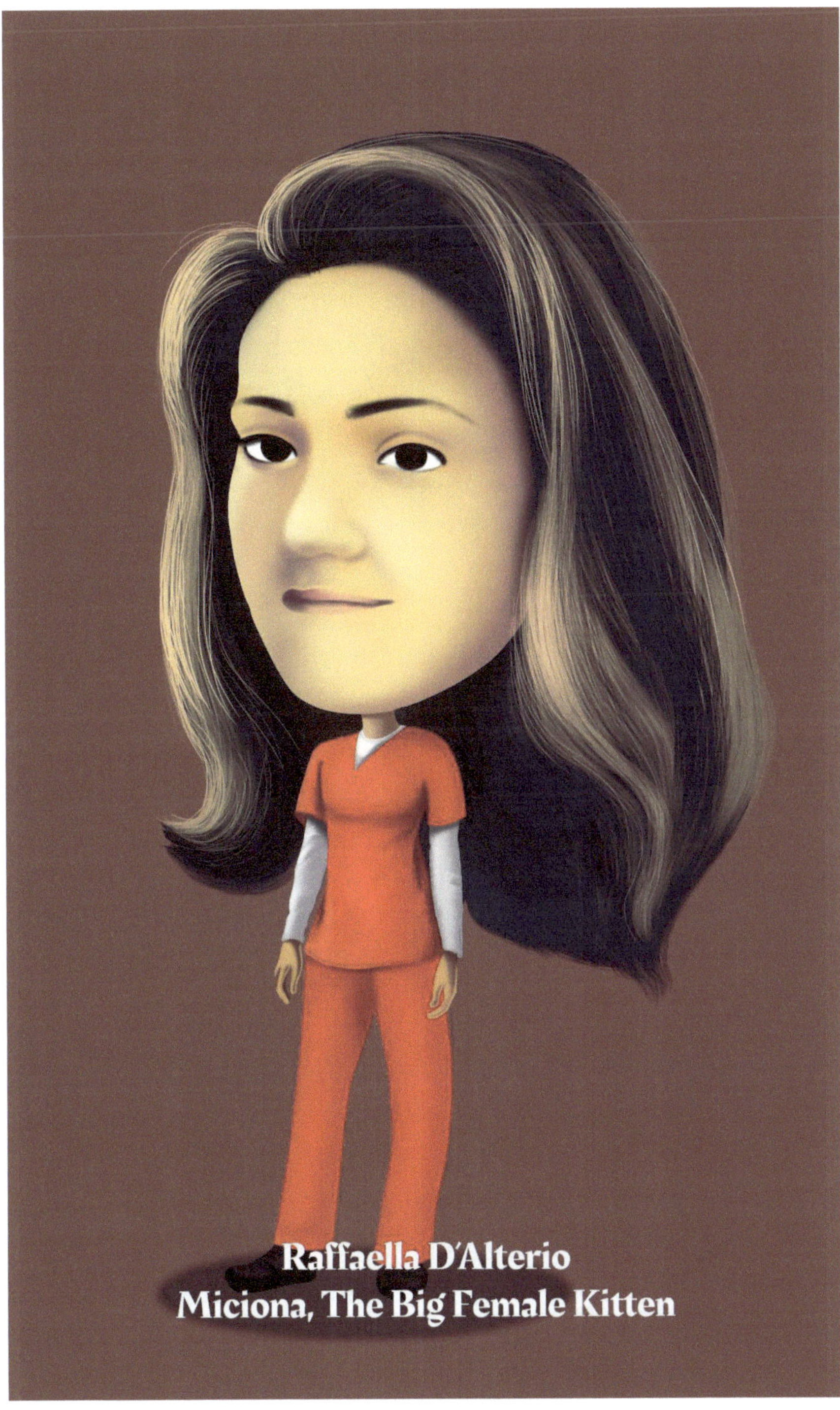

Raffaella D'Alterio
Miciona, The Big Female Kitten

Maria Licciardi
La Piccolina

In the eighties Gennaro Licciardi, known as *The Monkey,* was second in command to Luigi Giuliano for the Giuliano Clan. When Licciardi formed his own clan he centered his operations on the outskirts of Naples in Secondigliano, an area other clan leaders had no interest in. Licciardi turned the area into a vital center for the clan's drug trafficking and extortion operations. Licciardi's power and reach was extended when he became one of the founding members of the Secondigliano Alliance (SA) a group of Camorra clans that controlled the drug traffic and extortion rackets in the suburbs of Naples.

Gennaro Licciardi died in 1994 of blood poisoning while in Voghera prison, leaving the leadership of his clan to his two brothers Pietro and Vincenzo and his sister Maria, known as *La Piccolina* or *The Little One*. After Pietro and Vincenzo were arrested, Maria became the de facto leader of the clan. She was a natural boss not afraid of violence or breaking with traditional attitudes about what kind of businesses to be in, as long as there was a profit at the end of the day. Her leadership earned her the additional title of *Boss of Bosses*.

Maria resisted the initial violent attempts to wrestle control of the clan away from her, but she eventually consolidated her grip and extended her influence by forming alliances with twenty other Camorra clans that together controlled the drug, extortion, cigarette smuggling, and prostitution rackets. Prostitution was traditionally something the clans had stayed away from out of some peculiar macho attitude towards women, but Maria had no such aversion as long as it made money. Prostitution is a nasty violent business.

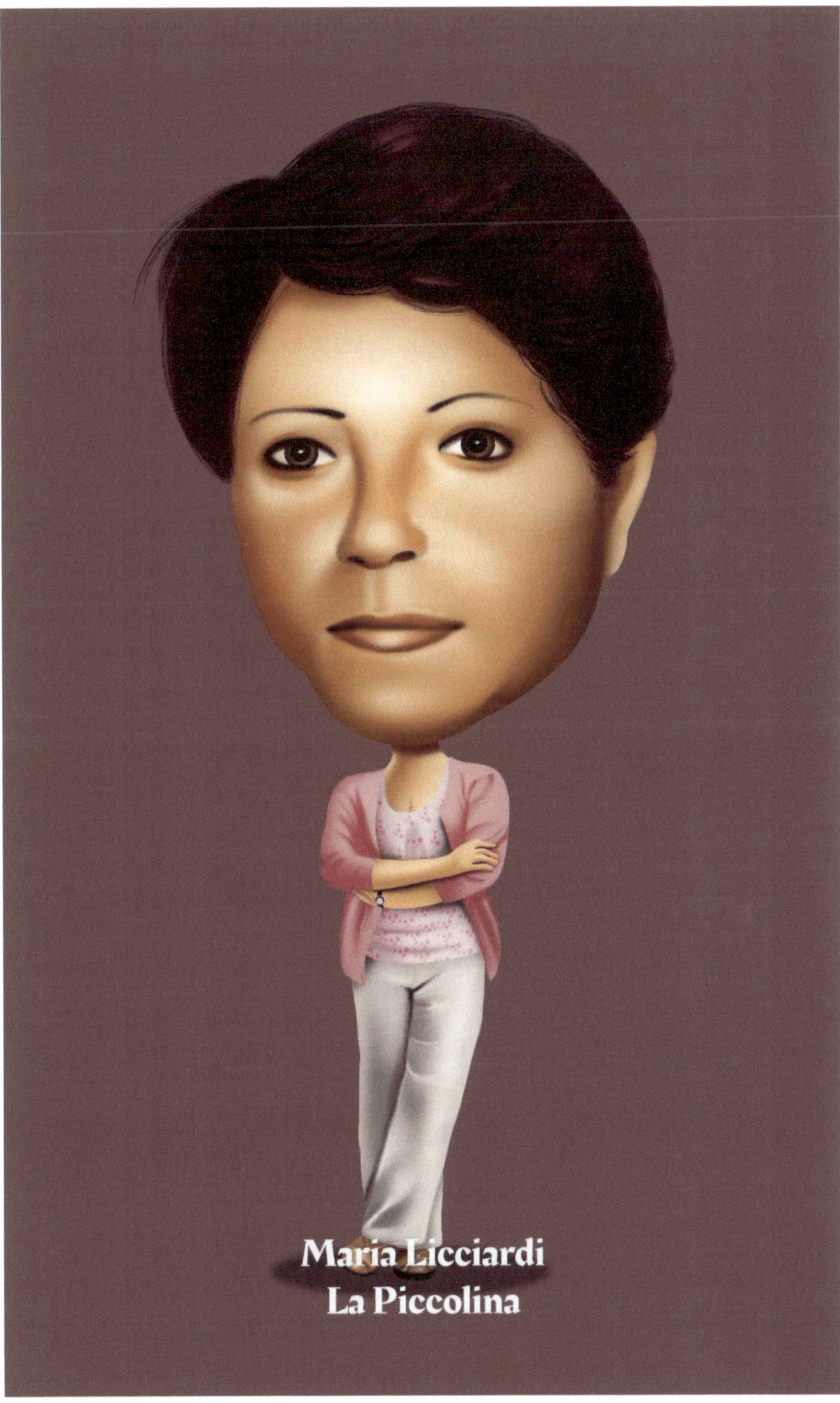

Maria Licciardi
La Piccolina

Young girls looking for a better life were purchased from the Albanian mafia, drugged, and forced into prostitution. When they got too old or their value diminished, they were murdered so they could never go to the police and become informants.

Like other mafia operations they provided jobs and charity to people in order to gain public acceptance. Unlike the Sicilian mafia that had some modicum of organizational discipline and structure, the Camorra clans ultimately always ended up in some sort of deadly feud. In 1999 the Alliance received a shipment of heroine that was so strong it was bound to kill many of the groups customers. Maria made the argument that selling the product was bad for business, but the La Russo Clan went ahead and sold the heroine anyway. Within one month, eleven people overdosed and died resulting in a police crackdown. The La Russo Clan broke away from the Alliance leading to an all-out war between the two groups. The feud resulted in one hundred and twenty people killed, forcing Maria Licciardi to go into hiding in a large abandoned warehouse attic complete with marble floors and a whirlpool. In an obviously flawed attempt to get the authorities to back off, she had her people bomb the district attorney's office. The strategy backfired with the police increasing their efforts to find and arrest her. It took two years but in 2001 she was finally caught and arrested. She continued to run the Licciari Clan while in jail.

Charmaine Roman
The Pot Queen

For twenty years Charmaine Roman lived illegally in central Florida operating a major Jamaican marijuana drug trafficking ring that

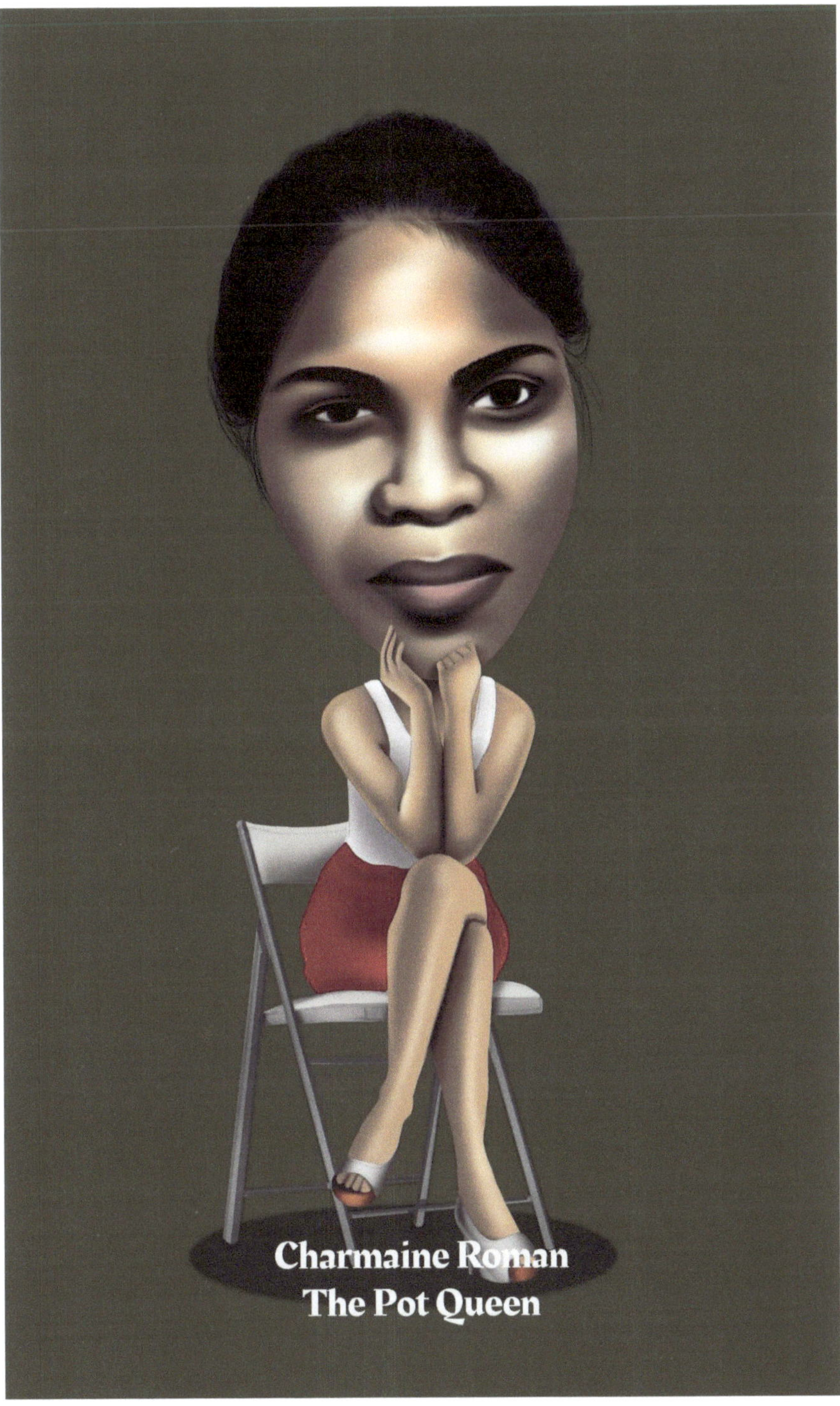

Charmaine Roman
The Pot Queen

grossed millions of dollars. Roman was the bookkeeping brains behind the operation using the concert promotion company *Sure Thing Investments* and her gambling pastime at the Wynn Casino in Las Vegas to launder the proceeds. From 2010 to 2012 Roman deposited over three million dollars at the Wynn Casino.

This wealthy high living central Florida grandmother was not only a clever enterprising criminal, she was also lucky: she cashed in forty-four state lottery scratch off tickets totalling one hundred and eighty-seven thousand dollars. One ticket alone was worth one hundred thousand dollars, but sooner or later good luck turns sour and things even out. Her high-roller lifestyle brought unwanted attention from both fellow criminals and the authorities. After winning fifteen thousand dollars on one scratch ticket, thieves broke into her condo, tied her and her daughter up, and demanded the winnings. But fellow criminals weren't her only problem; the police had been keeping an eye on her since 2006 without realizing she wasn't just a bookkeeper but the ringleader.

Roman was arrested in a police sting, *Operation Warehouse 13*, for trying to deliver four hundred pounds of marijuana at an Orlando parking lot. By the time of her arrest, her operation had smuggled thousands of pounds of pot. As part of the police sting, authorities recovered thirty-two hundred pounds of marijuana, two hundred thousand dollars' cash, fifteen illegal firearms, and several cars. The police sting resulted in fifty arrests. When arrested the police found Roman had several passports in different names, four Florida driver's licenses, and multiple Social Security cards. Roman and her colleagues were charged with racketeering, trafficking, and assorted other charges.

Jemeker Thompson
Queen Pin

Jemeker Thompson who became known as *Queen Pin* was a major
drug trafficker in Los Angeles in the 1980s. She started life as a poor
kid traumatized by an eviction from her home when she was still a
child. Without much in the way of opportunity or prospects, the
drug business seemed like a logical career path. She eventually
married an older fellow, Anthony "Daff" Mosley, and together they
had a son. Their partnership extended beyond marriage into a
working relationship that developed into a profitable cocaine
trafficking business. When crack appeared on the LA scene the pair
quickly adapted and became one of Los Angeles' top drug suppliers.
Their high profile operation was profitable, but the drug business
comes with a downside, ultimately leading to long prison terms or
worse. In the case of Daff Mosley it was the latter; he was shot dead
while washing his car.

Although Jemeker was saddened by the loss of her husband, the
father of her son, and her business partner, she continued in
business raking in the profits. She even diversified by investing in a
Los Angeles business that sold hair to celebrities. She travelled
around to shows promoting the product.

Meanwhile her drug trafficking business kept growing. She hooked
up with a man nicknamed *Cheese*. Cheese is a highly addictive form
of heroin made from a combination of Mexican black tar heroin and
Tylenol PM. The business continued to grow but like most high-
profile drug dealers, the end comes quickly. Cheese was arrested,
and being the lowlife that he was, he ratted on Jemeker. She went on
the lamb for two years, but in 1993 she decided to comeback to make
an appearance at her son's sixth grade graduation ceremony. She

was promptly arrested, convicted and sentenced to fifteen years in a maximum-security prison. In prison she found God and supposedly turned her life around, or alternatively found a new con. She was released in 2005 after serving thirteen years alongside fellow harpies Griselda Blanco and Manson groupie Squeaky Fromme.

Today Jemeker, *Queen Pin*, Thompson is an evangelical preacher with her own Second Chance Ministry in South Central, Los Angeles spreading the word to others of a second chance through God – praise the lord and pass the cheese.

Thelma Wright
Black Mafia Queen

Thelma Wright unlike most other drug dealers managed to eventually escape the life after making a fortune in the Philadelphia drug trade. One has to be sceptical of her pre-marriage description as just your average Catholic girl, after all, she did marry Jackie Wright a big time mover and shaker in the Philadelphia drug scene, and a member of the infamous Black Mafia known for killing cops. Her early life seemed normal enough raised in a wholesome environment with a good education, studying real estate management at Temple University. Wright is obviously smart and entrepreneurial. After moving to Los Angeles she started a clothing design company but she eventually tired of the LA scene and moved back to Philly.

Her relationship with gangster Jackie Wright could hardly be described as your normal good-girl dream match. The couple had a son in 1982 but by 1986 this average girl with the drug dealer husband was a widow. Jackie was found wrapped up in a rug with a bullet in his head. The new widow made a quick transition from

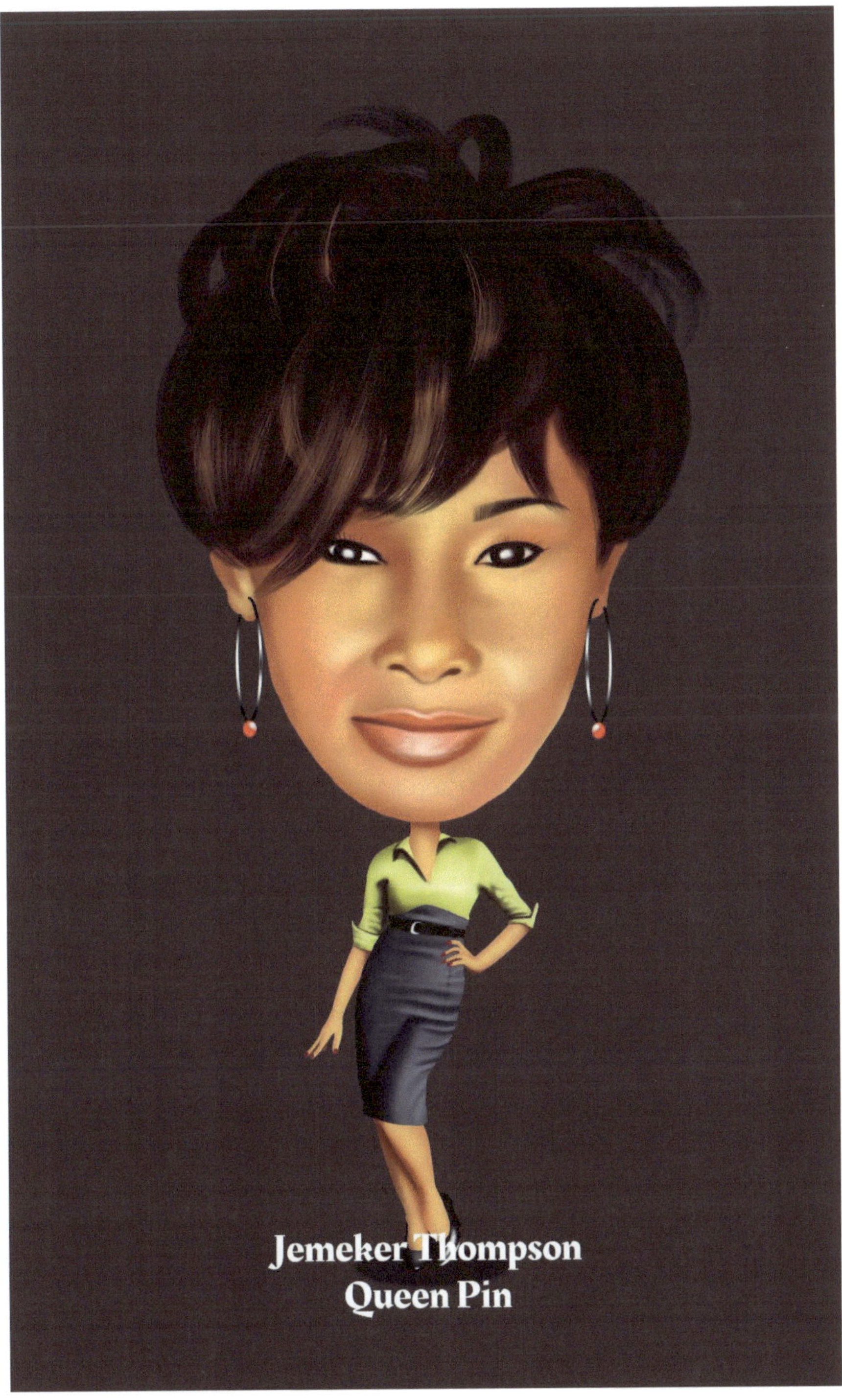

Jemeker Thompson
Queen Pin

housewife and mother to big time drug dealer by taking over her husband's business. Under her guidance the operation became the Philly supplier of heroin and cocaine, earning upwards of four hundred thousand dollars a month. Her tentacles reached all the way to Los Angeles moving large quantities of drugs between the two cities. She gained considerable respect from her fellow drug colleagues earning not one but two nicknames, *Queen Pen* and *Boss Lady*. Like I said , just your average widow looking out for her son.

The drug business is not without its downside and Wright did not escape the violent nature of the business as evidenced by her being in the wrong place at the wrong time when she and some friends were caught in a shootout at a Philadelphia nightclub. Within a couple of weeks of the shooting incident, one of her clients known as *Fats* was arrested when he complained to the Post Office about a missing package. It wasn't long after that she decided enough was enough and got out of the business before it caught up to her. Ironically, in retirement she worked for a non-profit organization for women dealing with addiction and mental health problems. After years of keeping a low profile she decided to write a book about her experiences, after all, a girl's got to make a living.

Shashikala Patankar
Baby The Meow-meow Queen

Shashikala was the youngest, and only girl, of seven children leading to her nickname *Baby*. While her brothers worked as drivers she earned a few rupees selling milk bottles in the South Mumbai slums. In 1985 she met a drug dealer offering a more profitable opportunity than selling milk bottles. Violence seemed to come easy to Baby, a trait that extended even to family if they didn't fall in line with her

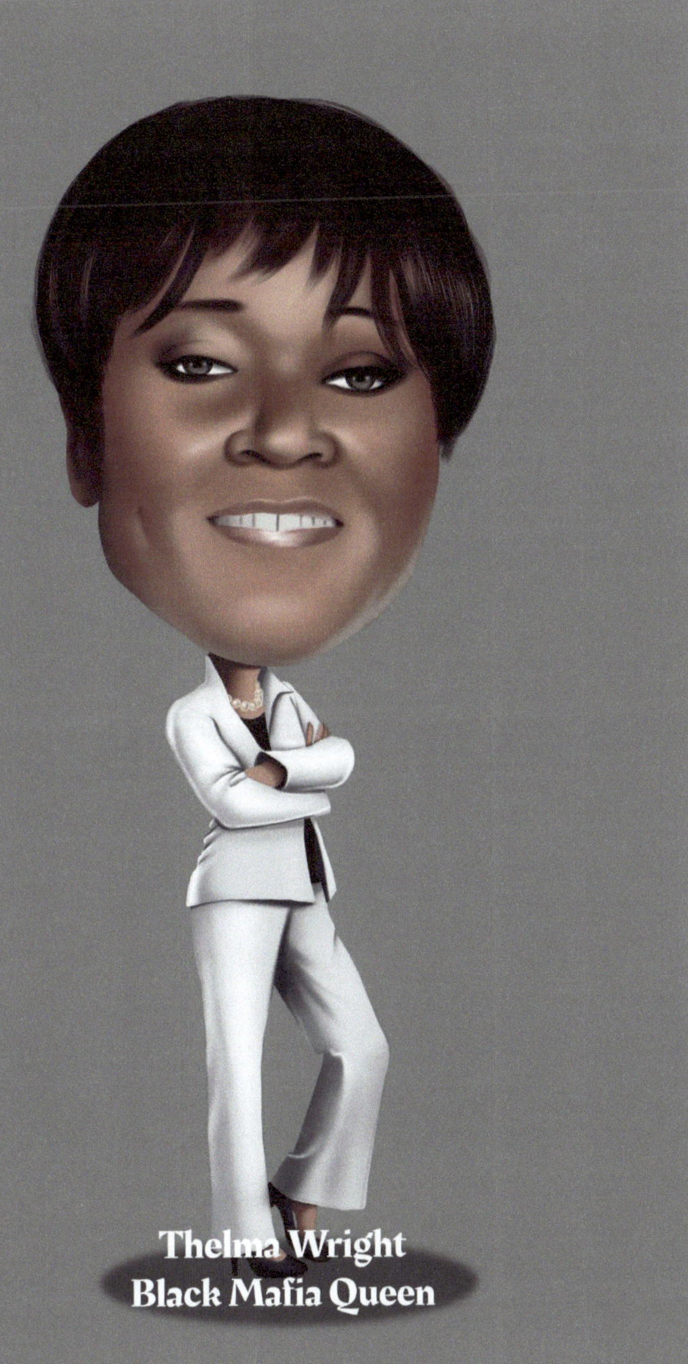

Thelma Wright
Black Mafia Queen

wishes. In 1992 her nephews accused *Baby* of burning their mother to death because she objected to Shashikala using her home to warehouse her drugs; however, narcotics officers claim the murder was the result of a drug feud between the two women.

Baby started out selling hashish and brown sugar from her hilltop home overlooking a slum area. She kept a low-profile remaining small-time flying under the police radar. Her efforts to stay out of trouble and expand her operation were enhanced when she was able to co-opt a policeman. She then switched to selling mephedrone, street-named *Meow-meow*, because it was cheaper, easily available, and at the time not covered under the Narcotic Drug and Psychotropic Substances (NDPS) Act.

The Police Anti Narcotics Cell made low-level arrests in the slums below Baby's hilltop home, but any time they climbed the hill to arrest Baby, someone alerted her, and each time she either escaped, or got rid of the drugs in her possession. It was during one of these raids that Baby met police constable Dharmaraj Kalokhe, whom she put on her payroll, and who was ultimately the link that led to her downfall. Kalokhe was able to transport the drugs in his bag and because he was travelling in an official police vehicle he was able to move freely around the area without concern for the system of checkpoints and roadblocks, called *nakabandis*.

Baby's drug business was able to provide her with substantial real estate holdings, a fleet of automobiles, and at least three bank accounts each with substantial sums of money. In March of 2015 police raided constable Dharmaraj Kalokhe's home and found 114 kg of mephedrone. He claimed Baby gave it to him for safekeeping and that it belonged to a Custom's official. The following day police

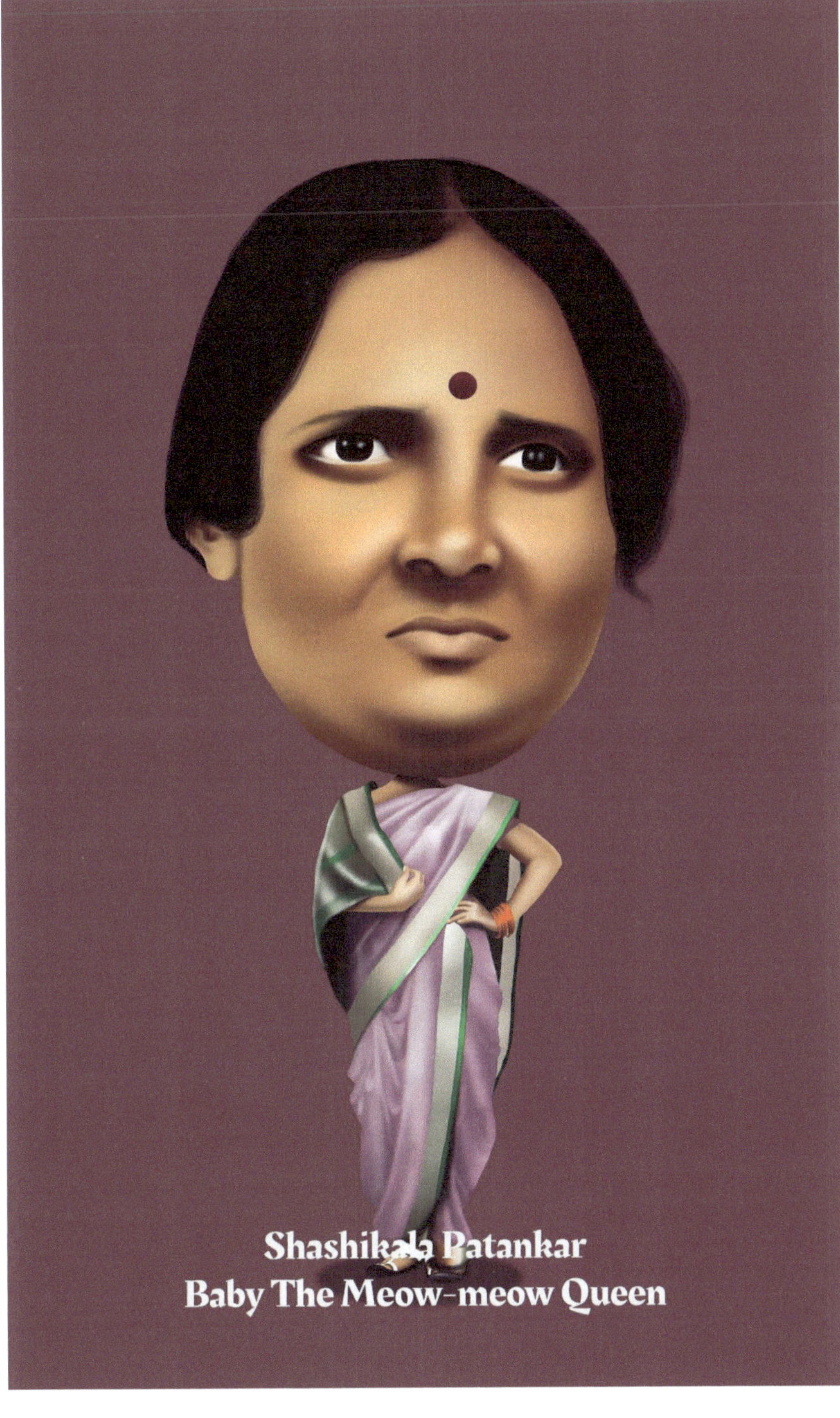

Shashikala Patankar
Baby The Meow-meow Queen

found another 12 kg of a suspicious substance in Kalokhe's police locker along with some cannabis and a stash of foreign currency. Several months later Baby was arrested but managed to obtain bail and disappear.

Police using phone records from one of her sons traced her movements to a home on the outskirts of Mumbai. Police questioned the woman who owned the home and found that Baby and two of her sons had fled to Surat and Delhi. Police teams were sent to both locations but the trail went cold. She and her sons were nowhere to be found.

Meanwhile Kalokhe who admitted his involvement with Baby tried to flee to his native village, Kanheri, but was found and arrested with a stash of mephedrone by an undercover team of police officers. Neighbours told the police a woman would show up at Kalokhe's home with a handkerchief hiding her face, and hand-over packages. The neighbour claimed Kalokhe would visit his native village quite often. An anonymous tip believed to have come from Baby herself prompted the police raid on Kalokhe's home. It seems Kalokhe decided to go into business on his own using the merchandise Baby gave him for safekeeping.

Rumour of police involvement in the drug business was an open secret and Kalokhe was merely a small player in the scheme of things. Baby was not one to be trifled with and if you crossed her she would get even. She had a history of informing the police on those that got in her way and her tips led to several high profile arrests in the police department not just Kalokhe.

Cheng Chui "Sister" Ping
Queen of the Snakeheads

The Black Societies or *Heishehui* are Chinese criminal gangs. Snakeheads are a particular kind of gang that specializes in smuggling people out of China into other countries. Sister Ping, as she was known, was one of the leading Snakehead leaders along with her partner, Guo Liang Chi, who went by the street name Ah Kay. The Snakehead gangs used stolen passports, illegal visas, business junkets, and tour groups to smuggle people out of China.

Ah Kay was leader of the violent *Fuk Ching* gang, one of the most powerful Chinese criminal organizations operating in New York City. Ah Kay and Sister Ping were central figures in the infamous *Golden Venture* smuggling disaster financed by Sister Ping. The *Golden Venture* was a cargo ship owned by Ping and used in an attempt to smuggle two hundred and eighty-six Chinese aliens into the United States in 1993. The scheme turned out to be a total disaster with a mutiny on board, the Captain held captive, and the ship running aground near Rockaway Beach in Queens, New York. Ten people drowned trying to make it to shore, with the remainder taken into custody by the U.S. Immigration and Nationalization Service, pending asylum or deportation.

Ah Kay was arrested in Hong Kong and extradited to the United States. In return for a lighter sentence Ah Kay became a witness for the government leading to the prosecution of numerous Chinatown gang members. When Sister Ping was arrested in 2005 for smuggling illegal immigrants and money laundering, her old partner Ah Kay testified against her. Sister Ping charged as much as $40,000 per head to smuggle people into the United States. If people couldn't pay, they were forced to work off their debt. Ah Kay was responsible for making sure everybody paid.

If the *Golden Venture* deal had been successful it would have grossed Ping and Ah Kay an estimated eight and a half million dollars. Sister Ping didn't regard the *Golden Venture* scheme as a particularly important operation; human smuggling wasn't considered her main moneymaking operation despite the fact she managed to smuggle some three thousand people into the United States, grossing about forty million dollars.

In addition to her smuggling activities she owned restaurants, a clothing store, and real estate holdings in China, Hong Kong, and South Africa. Investigations revealed her main money making operation was an underground banking network with tentacles in New York, Thailand, Singapore, Hong Kong, and China. Her smuggling career started in 1984 and lasted until the year 2000 when she was arrested. She died in prison in 2014 from cancer.

Ping was born in 1949 in the village of Shengmei, a poor farming town, just months before Mao Zedong established the People's Republic of China. As a youngster she went to the local school while working on the family farm raising pigs and rabbits, chopping wood, and looking after a vegetable garden. During Mao's Cultural Revolution she became the leader in her village for the infamous Red Guard. Ping's father became a merchant marine managing to sneak into the United States where he worked for thirteen years sending money back home before he was caught and deported back to China. On his return he got into the smuggling business. Ping eventually married, had three children, and in 1981 managed to make her way to New York City's Chinatown where she opened the Tak Shun

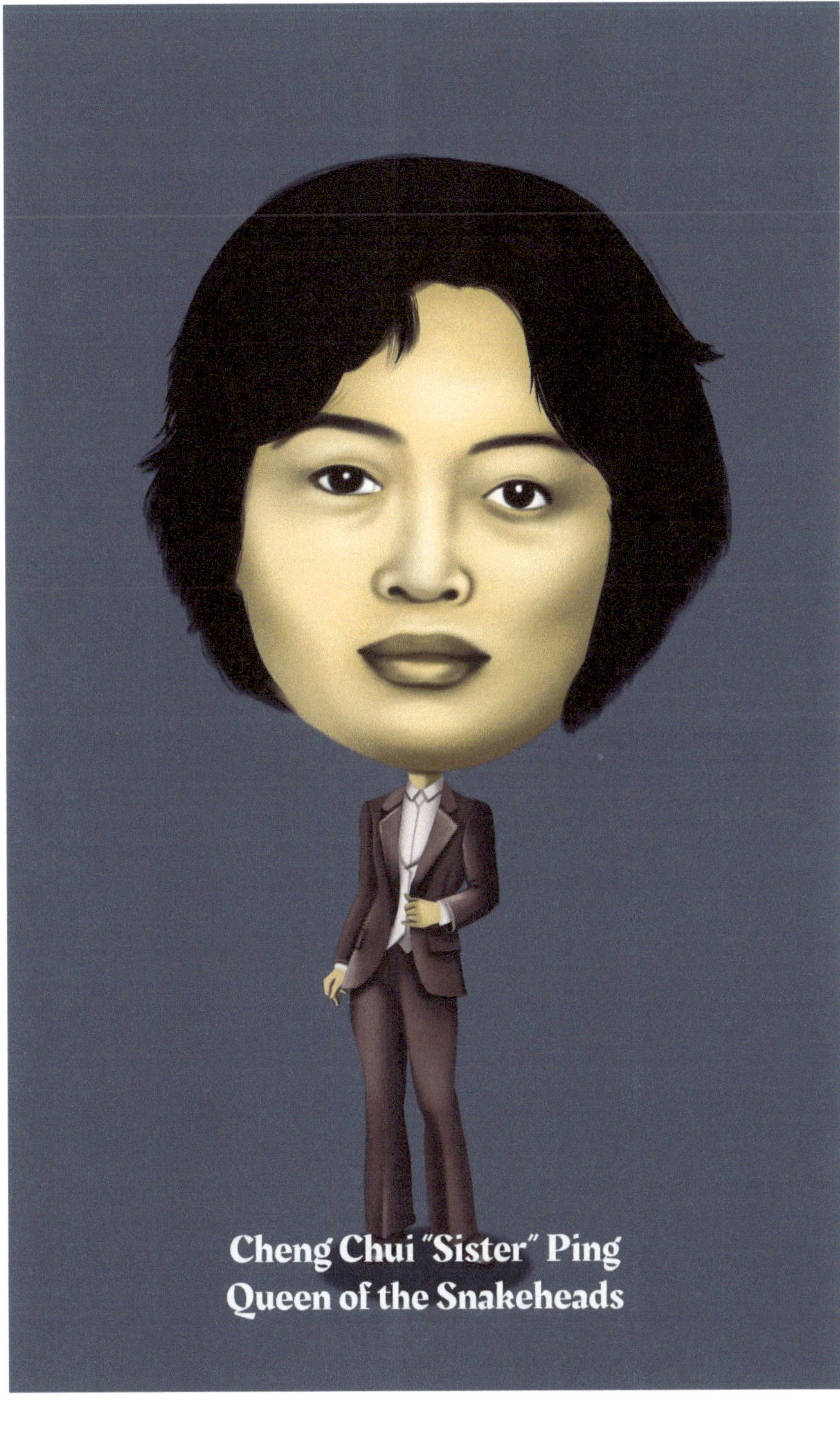

Cheng Chui "Sister" Ping
Queen of the Snakeheads

Variety Store targeting people from her home province of Fujian.

In the early 1980s she expanded into smuggling. It began as a one-woman operation smuggling small numbers of villagers from China to the United States using counterfeit documents in order to avoid the authorities. Business started booming after the Tiananmen Square massacre when the United States made it easier for Chinese students to stay in the country. Thousands of illegal immigrants started to arrive hoping to take advantage of the new rules.

As her smuggling empire grew she partnered with Ah Kay, leader of the *Fuk Ching* gang, a violent Chinese criminal gang in order to force people to pay what they owed. She also established her profitable underground banking network out of her Tak Shun Variety Store. After the *Golden Venture* fiasco, she fled to China because it doesn't have an extradition treaty with the United States. She was eventually arrested in Hong Kong in 2000, extradited to the U.S. where she stood trial and was sentenced to thirty-five years in prison for smuggling, hostage-taking, money laundering, and trafficking in ransom proceeds.

The *Golden Venture*, renamed the *United Caribbean*, was eventually purchased by Palm Beach County in 2000, and sunk one mile off the south Florida coast near the Boca Raton Inlet as part of the Palm Beach Artificial Reef Program.

Xie Caiping
Godmother of the Underworld

Sister Ping wasn't the only Chinese female gangster to make a big splash and ultimately end up serving a lengthy prison sentence. Xie

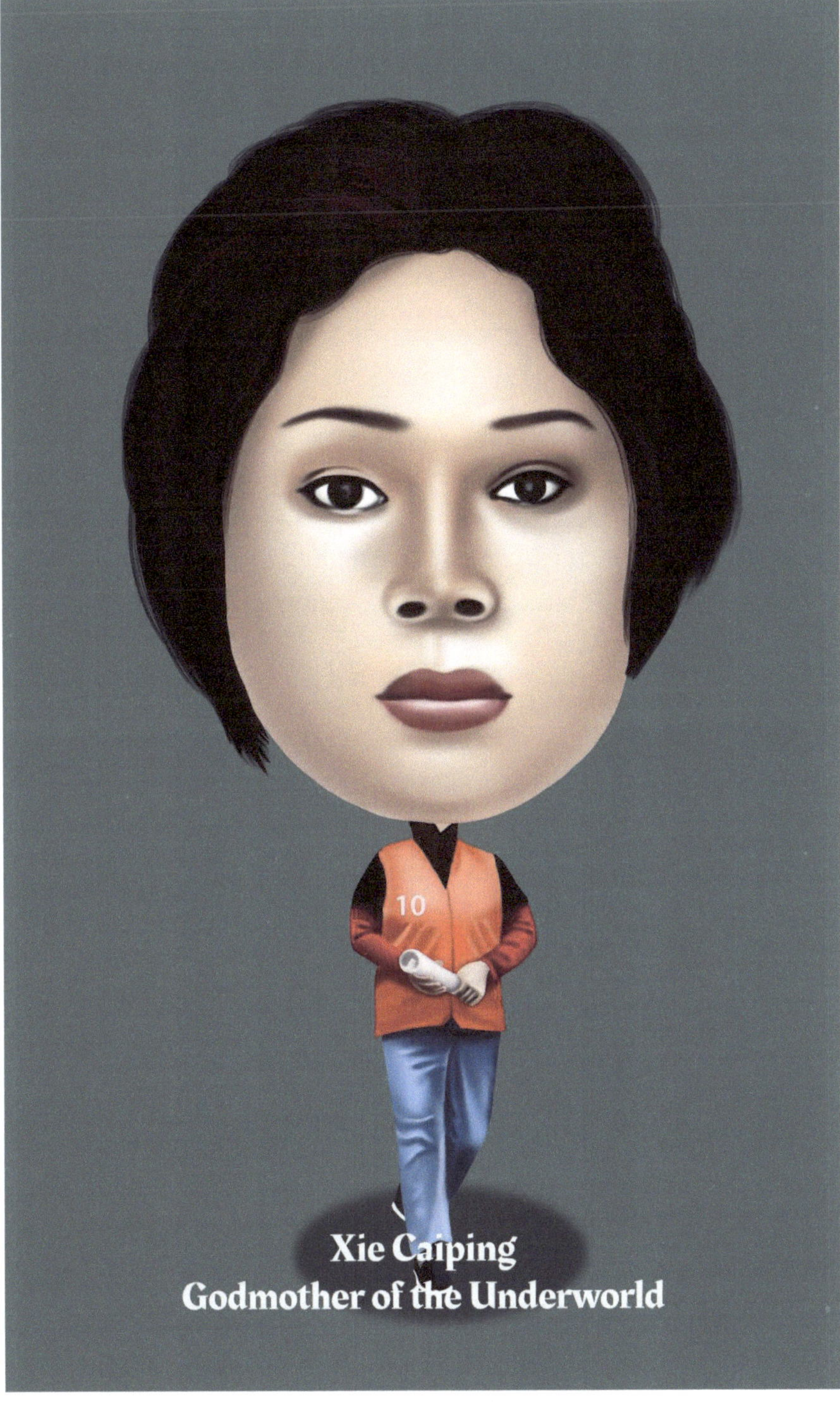

Xie Caiping
Godmother of the Underworld

Caiping, Godmother of the Underworld, was the head of a black society (heishehui) working out of the south-western city of Chongqing where her bother-in-law, Wen Qiang, just happened to be the city's Deputy Police Chief and Director of its Justice Bureau, that is, until his arrest for a myriad of offences including protecting his sister-in-law's illegal activities.

If there is any doubt that women are just as violent as men when in charge of a criminal operation, all one has to do is a take a look at the career of Xie Caiping. She used whatever violent means was necessary, including the beating of a police officer, in order to keep the profits flowing from her gambling operation. Her reputation for excess is legendary with rumours that she had as many as sixteen lovers although police claim the middle aged gangster only had one twenty-six-year-old boy toy.

With her brother-in-law as Deputy Police Chief she was able to operate with impunity. He would warn her of any impending police raids allowing her time to grab whatever cash she could lay her hands on and disappear until the coast was clear. So brazen was her activities that one of her gambling dens was located in a hotel across the road from the Chongqing courthouse and next to the local prosecutor's office. Her gambling operations brought in hundreds of thousands of dollars.

Xie was convicted and sentenced to eighteen years in prison for operating a criminal syndicate, running a string of gambling dens, illegal imprisonment, taking illegal drugs, and bribing government officials. Xie's arrest was part of a major crackdown in Chongqing that netted numerous criminals sentenced to long prison terms, and in some cases death sentences. Fourteen high-ranking public officials along with numerous prominent business leaders were also caught in the crackdown.

Organized crime seems to flourish in the decentralized Chinese system that includes five layers of government with local officials wielding significant independent authority.

Bōsōzoku
暴走族

Every country at one time or another has had their share of trouble with motorcycle gangs, but like almost everything else, the Japanese manage to add an extra dash of style and panache when it comes to their variations of youth culture and juvenile delinquency. Young Japanese women seem to relish the idea of being outrageous and in your face when it comes to expressions of counterculture angst and protest. In order to place the *Bosozoku* motorcycle gang girls in context perhaps it's best to start with several other bizarre teenage female expressions of protest. The first in a long list of crazy girl trends is the *Gyaru*, a name derived from the English word *gal* or *girl* adapted from a 1970s brand of Japanese jeans called *gurls*.

 The *Gyaru* are teenage girls that dye their hair outlandish colors, apply bizarre white makeup on their lips and around their eyes over a disturbingly unnatural-looking tan. There are notable subgroups of the *Gyaru* with each screwier than the next, the *Hime gyaru*, or *Hime-kei*, are one of the more out-there subculture variants. We're talking about a fashion style that would make Bozo the Clown cringe. This variation of girl-crazy seems to combine the fashion sense of Clarabelle with an eighteenth century Rococo hooker. They wear skirts or dresses in pink or pastel colors accessorized with lace and bows. Their wildly colored bouffant hairstyles seem to have been created in a wind tunnel rather than a beauty salon. This group also tends to decorate their homes in a similarly extreme manner; all-in-all these girls tend to pursue a persona of Little Bo Peep on a bad psychedelic trip.

There are almost as many subgroups and variations of the Gyaru as there are variations of electronic music, and that's a lot. Beyond the *Gyaru* there are other non-*Gyaru* groups like the *Lolita* girls who look like life-sized Victorian dress-up dolls: that's Queen Victoria, not Victoria's Secret. Japanese counterculture street fashion looks like Salvador Dali and Pablo Picasso were let loose in Japan with unlimited supplies of paint, and orders to decorate everyone under the age of eighteen; but let's get back to the *Bosozoku* gangs, a group with their own unique sense of style and protest.

Bosozoku literally means *violent or out-of-control tribes*. These motorcycle gangs date back to the post WWII era when they were known as *kaminari zoku* (thunder tribes) with members coming from the socially disaffected lower economic classes. It was a way for estranged youth to protest the restrictive and socially limiting nature of conventional Japanese society.

The *Bosozoku* girls opt for a distinctive fashion style that combines the look of a WWII U.S. Navy uniform and a Kamikaze jumpsuit, complete with gang colors and markings. Alternatively, they'll wear a long jacket called a *tokko-fuku* (Special Attack Uniform) with matching baggy pants tucked into retro pilot boots, and of course the obligatory gang insignia. Decorating their uniforms and bikes doesn't seem to be enough so they have long painted multi-colored

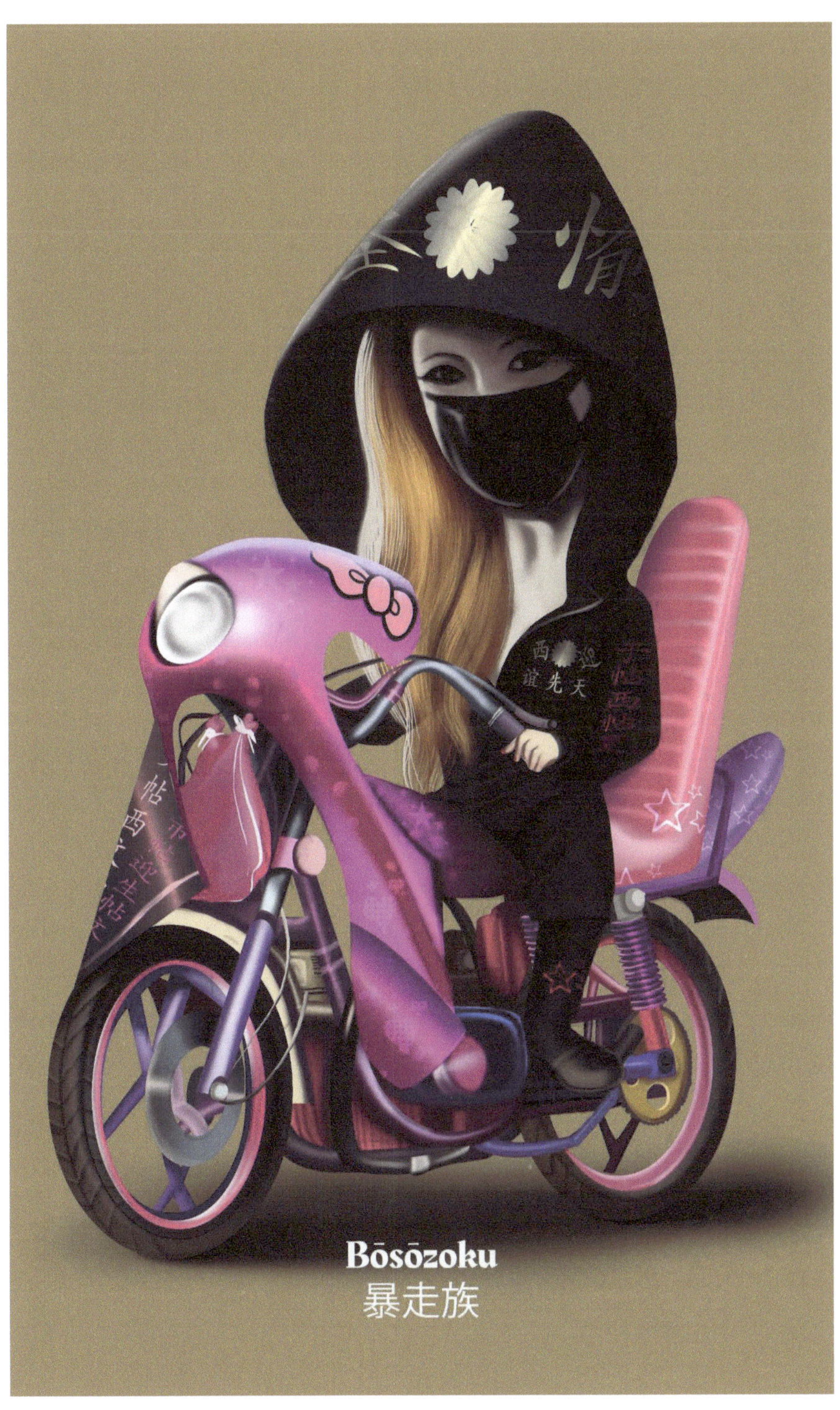

Bōsōzoku

暴走族

fingernails and tattoos, all in a cultural slap-in-the-face to traditional Japanese mores.

Their bizarrely modified bikes or scooters are painted in bright colors often pink or red with flowers. The handlebars are adjusted down and inward so they can easily weave in and out of traffic while yelling at pedestrians and waving Imperial Japanese flags or metal pipes in what the police call *Maru-Sō*. They've even been known to beat up bystanders that protest their antics, and sometimes-even use Molotov cocktails when the occasion calls for more extreme measures. One of their favorite games is to clog the streets with large numbers of gang members revving their engines making as much noise as possible in order to disturb the neighbourhood. They usually don't wear helmets, run red lights, and break as many traffic laws as possible.

The popularity of the Bosozoku reached its height in the early 1980s when memberships in the various gangs hit a high of more than forty-two thousand. In recent years their numbers have shrunk to under ten thousand but they are still around making a cultural statement with their style and behavior. The Bosozoku girls are fond of flaunting their antisocial antics designed to disrupt traditional Japanese female stereotypes, saying 'Japanese women can wipe their own asses'.

References

- theguardiam.com, Girl gang's grip London underworld revealed
- www.dailymail.co.uk/femail/article-1342450/Female-shoplifters-ransacked-West-End-shops-hid-loot-knickerbockers.html
- www.mandatory.com/2015/05/01/the-10-most-insane-criminal-moms/
- en.wikipedia.org/wiki/Kate_Leigh
- en.wikipedia.org/wiki/Sly-grog_shop
- en.wikipedia.org/wiki/Razor_gang
- en.wikipedia.org/wiki/Tilly_Devine
- evilladies.com/just-plain-evil/tilly-devine-and-kate-leigh-razor-gang/
- en.wikipedia.org/wiki/Nellie_Cameron
- Stylist.co.uk History's most notorious female criminals
- Listverse.com, 10 Of The Richest And Most Powerful Female Crime Lords Ever
- sallyjling.org/2011/06/28/gertrude-lythgoe-fascinating-women-of-prohibition/
- www.bahamapundit.com/2007/09/heres-to-the-bo.html
- sallyjling.org/marie-waite-spanish-marie/
- www.forbes.com/sites/nathanielparishflannery/2015/02/09/mexicos-organized-crime-queenpin-released-from-prison/
- en.wikipedia.org/wiki/Miguel_Ángel_Félix_Gallardo
- en.wikipedia.org/wiki/Domino_Harvey
- www.telegraph.co.uk/news/obituaries/1493030/Domino-Harvey.html
- thetalko.com 15 Most Dangerous Female Gangsters In The World, by Courtney Hardwick
- www.dailymail.co.uk/news/article-2650616/Mexican-Kim-Kardashian-lookalike-takes-boss-drug-cartel-hit-squad-uses-personalised-pink-AK47.html
- en.wikipedia.org/wiki/Los_Ántrax
- www.thefix.com/content/10-sexiest-drug-smugglers-and-traffickers
- www.biography.com/people/lisette-lee-21241483
- bangkok.coconuts.co/2014/06/12/former-sexy-model-yuyee-gets-15-years-smuggling-coke
- en.wikipedia.org/wiki/Rosetta_Cutolo
- en.wikipedia.org/wiki/Camorra
- www.theaustralian.com.au/news/penthouse-pet-simone-farrow-unfit-to-face-trial-due-to-potential-psychosis/story-e6frg6n6-1226582104034
- www.dailymail.co.uk/news/article-3019826/Former-swimsuit-model-Penthouse-Pet-accused-running-international-drug-ring-Hollywood-importing-meth-Australia-cries-court-talks-addiction-drugs.html

• en.wikipedia.org/wiki/Angie_Sanclemente_Valencia

•www.vancouversun.com/business/Aspiring+Playboy+model+from+Vancouver+behind+bars+after+California+drug+bust/10296643/story.html?__lsa=f8ce-e21b

• www.dailymail.co.uk/news/article-2164907/Raffaella-DAlterio-Female-Mafia-boss-known-The-Big-Female-Kitten-arrest.html

• en.wikipedia.org/wiki/Camorra

• www.dailymail.co.uk/news/article-2477999/Florida-drug-kingpin-grandmother-laundered-millions-dollars-won-187-000-scratch-lottery-tickets-2010.html

• www.biography.com/people/jemeker-thompson-21040767

• en.wikipedia.org/wiki/Anna_Chapman

• en.wikipedia.org/wiki/Illegals_Program

• www.telegraph.co.uk/news/worldnews/europe/russia/7866823/MI5-investigates-KGB-father-of-Russian-spy.html

• indianexpress.com/article/india/india-others/the-sunday-story-meow-meow-and-baby/

• www.vagabomb.com/The-Most-Dangerous-Women-Criminals-of-The-th-Century/

• Mentalfloss.com 10 Female Gangsters You Should Know About

• thepenhustler.com/2015/02/05/stephanie-st-clair/

• en.wikipedia.org/wiki/Stephanie_St._Clair

• listverse.com/2014/09/12/10-of-the-richest-and-most-powerful-female-crime-lords-ever/

• www.biography.com/people/thelma-wright-21241567

• en.wikipedia.org/wiki/Licciardi_clan

• https://en.wikipedia.org/wiki/Maria_Licciardi

• theguardian.com/world/2009/nov/03/china-jails-godmother-underworld

• economist.com/node/14539628

• gothamist.com/2013/01/18/notorious_female_mobsters.php

• en.wikipedia.org/wiki/Sister_Ping

• en.wikipedia.org/wiki/Golden_Venture

• en.wikipedia.org/wiki/Laura_Bullion

• en.wikipedia.org/wiki/William_Carver_(Wild_Bunch)

• en.wikipedia.org/wiki/Butch_Cassidy%27s_Wild_Bunch

• en.wikipedia.org/wiki/Ann_Bassett

• en.wikipedia.org/wiki/Pearl_Elliott

• dailymail.co.uk/femail/article-2594830/Japanese-Bosozoku-bikie-gang-girls-bad-ass-feminine.html

• en.wikipedia.org/wiki/Bōsōzoku
• cracked.com/article_18567_6-japanese-subcultures-that-are-insane-even-japan.html
• en.wikipedia.org/wiki/Gyaru
• mookychick.co.uk/indie-fashion/vintage/bosozoku-japanese-biker-gangs-and-bosozoku-style-2.php
• independent.co.uk/news/world/americas/mexicos-most-infamous-female-drugs-cartel-leader-is-arrested-after-boyfriend-turns-her-in-a6678766.html
• independent.co.uk/news/world/americas/mexicos-most-infamous-female-drugs-cartel-leader-is-arrested-after-boyfriend-turns-her-in-a6678766.html
• cracked.com/blog/5-strange-real-life-gangs-that-put-the-warriors-to-shame/

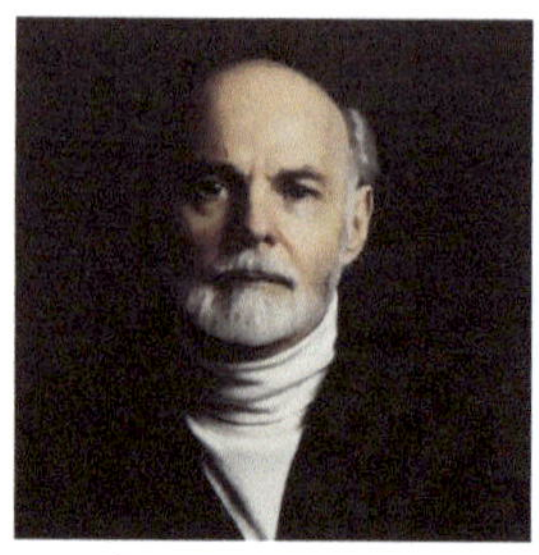

Author Biography

Jerry Bader is Senior Partner at MRPwebmedia.com a small media production company that specializes in Web video, audio, music, and sound design. He is responsible for developing concepts for clients' video campaigns, writing the scripts, and managing the production process. Over the years he's written over a hundred articles on marketing, and he's self-published three marketing e-books and a couple of free e-magazines. Currently he has turned his attention to writing a number of Neo Noir Hybrid Graphic Novels and story concepts with the goal of turning them into television series or feature films. There are currently ten screenplays in The Method series.

The Method Graphic Novel has been chosen by Blurb to be used has an example of what can be done with cross-platform multimedia book publishing and was featured at Comic-Con. He has also written a novel, *The Fixer* that is being published by Rebel Seed Entertainment. *The Fixer* is based on the true-life story of a colorful horse racing character. He is also working with Film Producer, Laura Cross of Rebel Seed Entertainment to turn The Fixer into a Limited Television Series. For more information: http://www.rebelseedentertainment.com/project-thefixer/.

The Method and *The Comeuppance* are both available on Blurb in print and ebook formats.

The Method
eBook Version: http://bit.ly/1D934yA
Print Versions: http://bit.ly/1EHJaaf

The Comeuppance
eBook Version: http://bit.ly/1TqX6Tb
Print Version: http://bit.ly/1DO1apo

Graphic Novels Available: and Coming

The Method

A down-and-out LA actor with a knack for impersonations finds his circumstances
completely reversed by a chance meeting with a look-alike stranger.

Synopsis

A down-and-out LA actor with a knack for impersonations finds his circumstances
completely reversed by a chance meeting with a look-alike stranger. After a night
of drinking with his new friend discussing the possibilities made possible by their
similar appearance, the stranger offers the actor a ride home. On the way there is
an accident and one of them is killed. The survivor finds himself in the hospital
with amnesia and everyone assuming he's the stranger, the right-hand man for a
mob boss. The survivor plays the role that's expected of him, despite the fact that
doubt about who he is, weighs heavy on his mind. Life becomes a balancing act
between the role he finds himself playing and the search for who he really is: the
down-and-out actor or the mob *consigliere*?

The Comeuppance

When mob boss, Carmine DeSalvo, finds out his accident-prone, amnesiac right-
hand man, Arnie Bernardo, isn't who he thinks he is; when he decides Arnie's girl,
Lonnie, is too tempting to resist; and when hit men, Vito and Sid, figure Carmine
is past his best before date; somebody ends up dead. Meanwhile Seymour Kratz,
the guy running the mob's movie operation, is skimming, and something has to be
done. In the end, somebody always dies. The question is, who is it going to be?

The Fixer (A Biography)

Published By Rebel Seed Entertainment

The true life story of a son of a concentration camp survivor left to fend for
himself using his wit, charm, and guts to survive and prosper as a jockey, trainer,
and fixer of horse races all while navigating through an environment populated by
gamblers, gangsters, and billionaires.

Available on Amazon: http://amzn.to/1ZoJCMe

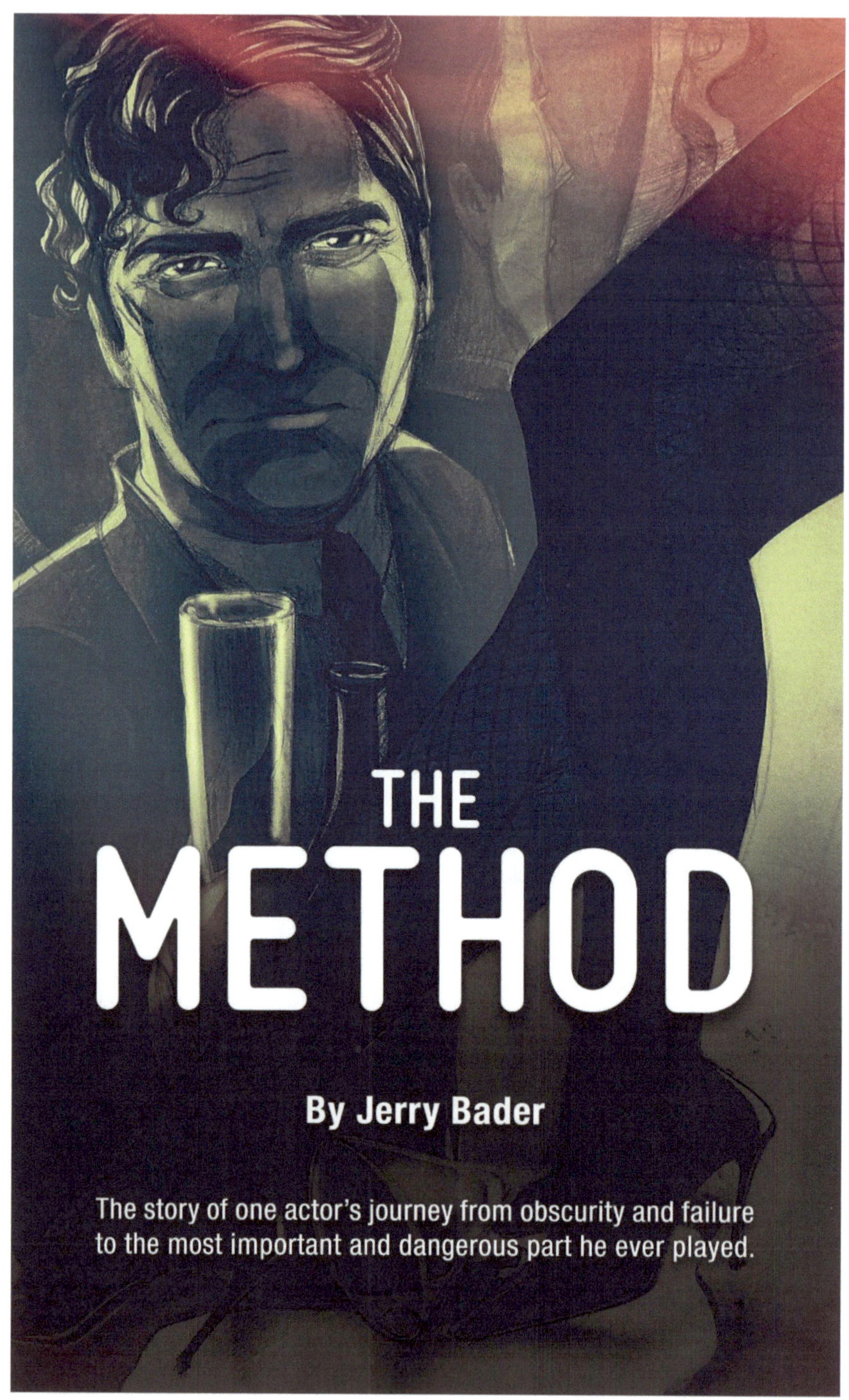

The Method
eBook Version: http://bit.ly/1D934yA
Print Versions: http://bit.ly/1EHJaaf

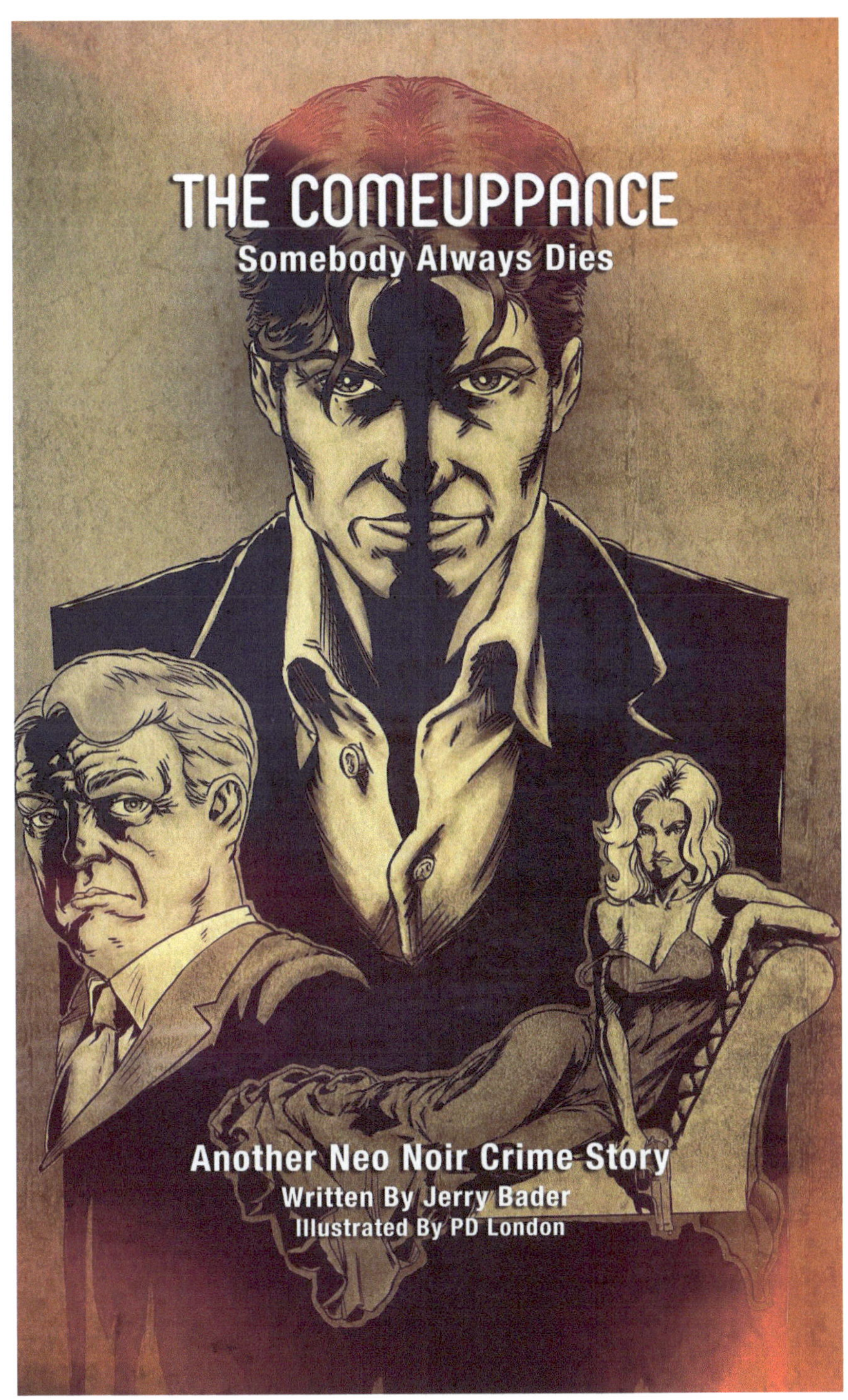

The Comeuppance
eBook Version: http://bit.ly/1TqX6Tb
Print Version: http://bit.ly/1DO1apo

THE FIXER

BY JERRY BADER

A COLLECTION OF TALES FROM THE LIFE OF A NOTORIOUS JOCKEY AND HIS EXPLOITS AMONGST THE DANGEROUS GANGSTERS, DEGENERATE GAMBLERS, CROOKED POLITICIANS, AND CORRUPT BILLIONAIRES OF THE HORSE RACING WORLD

Available on Amazon: http://amzn.to/1ZoJCMe

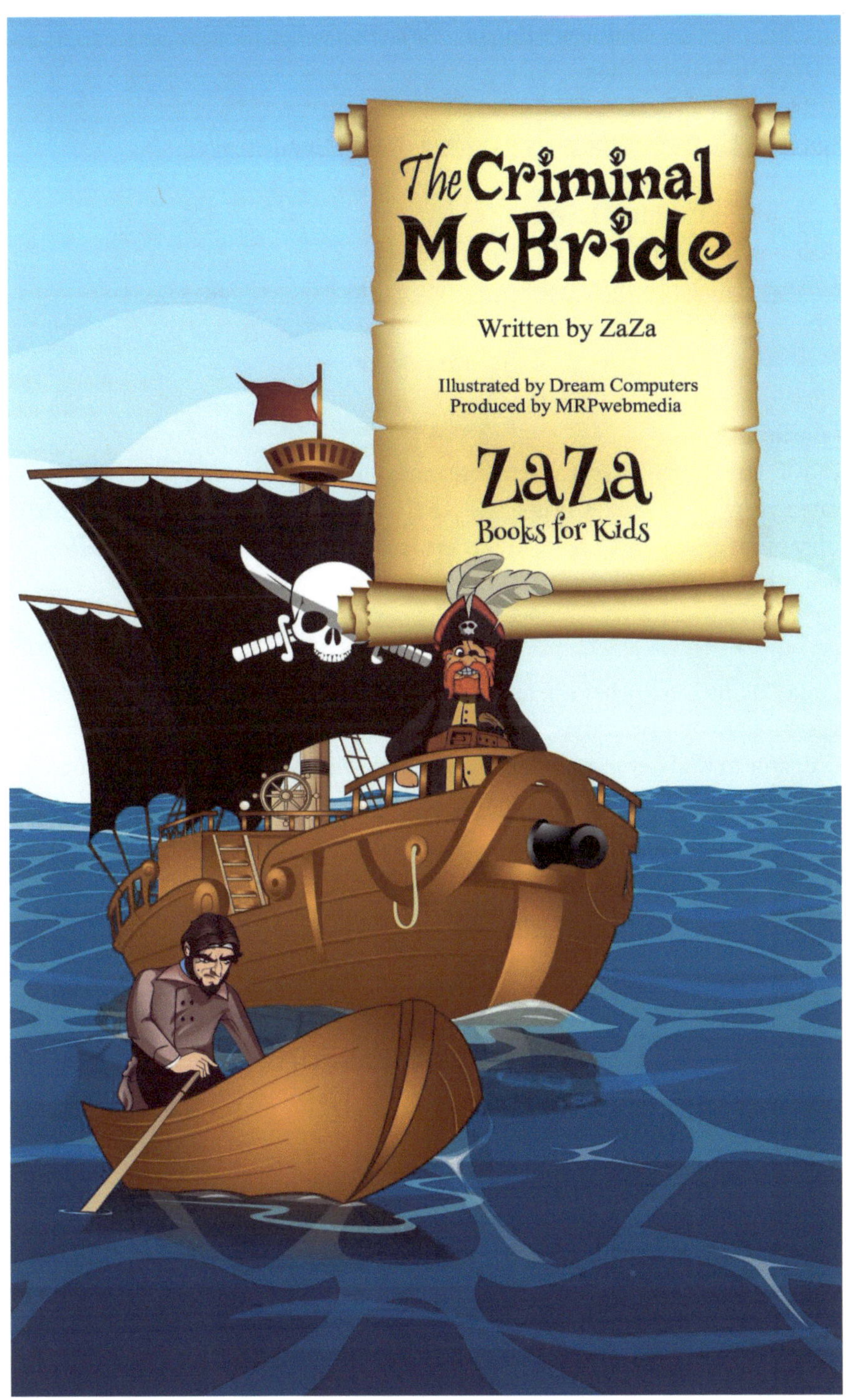

The Tale of The Criminal McBride
Available on Blurb in ebook and print formats:
http://www.blurb.com/b/7229938-the-criminal-mcbride?ebook=587454

Coming Soon

The Coffin Corner
A beautiful psychiatrist with a heart-breaking childhood hires a second rate
Private Eye, with an equally tragic past, to find her missing husband. The husband
has disappeared without a trace or any evidence of ever existing despite being
gainfully employed as a bartender.

Synopsis
Virginia Collins is not what she appears to be. By all outward appearances the
successful uptown psychiatrist is just another beautiful dame who hires a private
investigator to find her missing husband: a weird little man who makes fancy
umbrella drinks and dresses like something out of a old gangster movie. Collins
hides her real motives, along with her tragic past in order to win the affections of
Raffy Rheinhardt, a cynical PI with an equally tragic history; a long forgotten
shared incident resulting in damaged psyches and dead bodies.

Caught in the middle is the stunning Charlene (Charlie) Coffin, heiress to a
distillery fortune, the remainder of which is The Coffin Building that houses the
bizarre Dystopia Bar and the office of R.R. Rheinhardt. Despite being Raffy's
landlord, Charlie works with Raffy as his assistant, not just because she finds the
work exciting; but also because she loves him, an issue that doesn't go down well
with the disturbed blonde psychiatrist client.

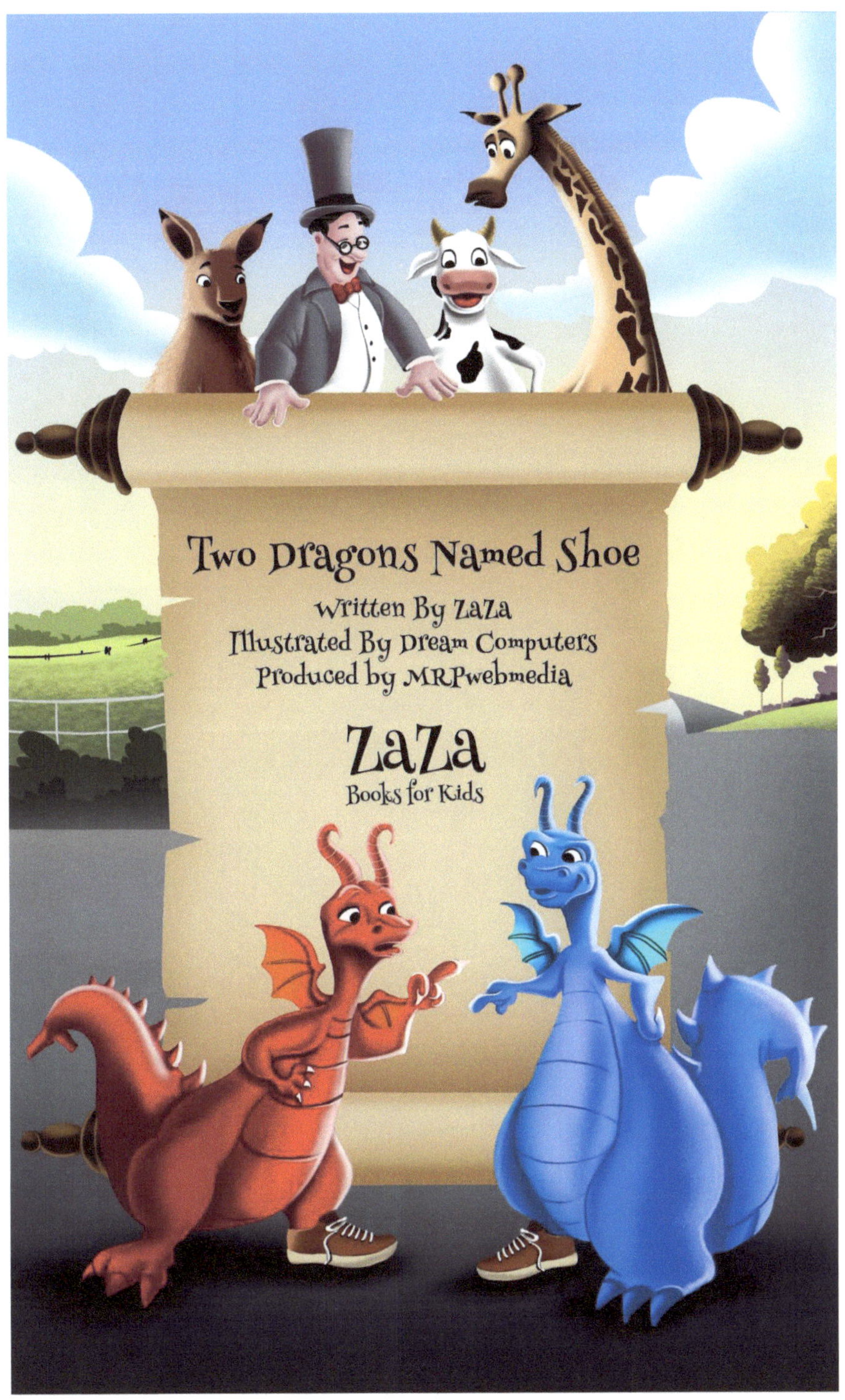

Two Dragons Named Shoe
Available on Blurb in ebook and print formats:
http://www.blurb.com/ebooks/577412-two-dragons-named-shoe

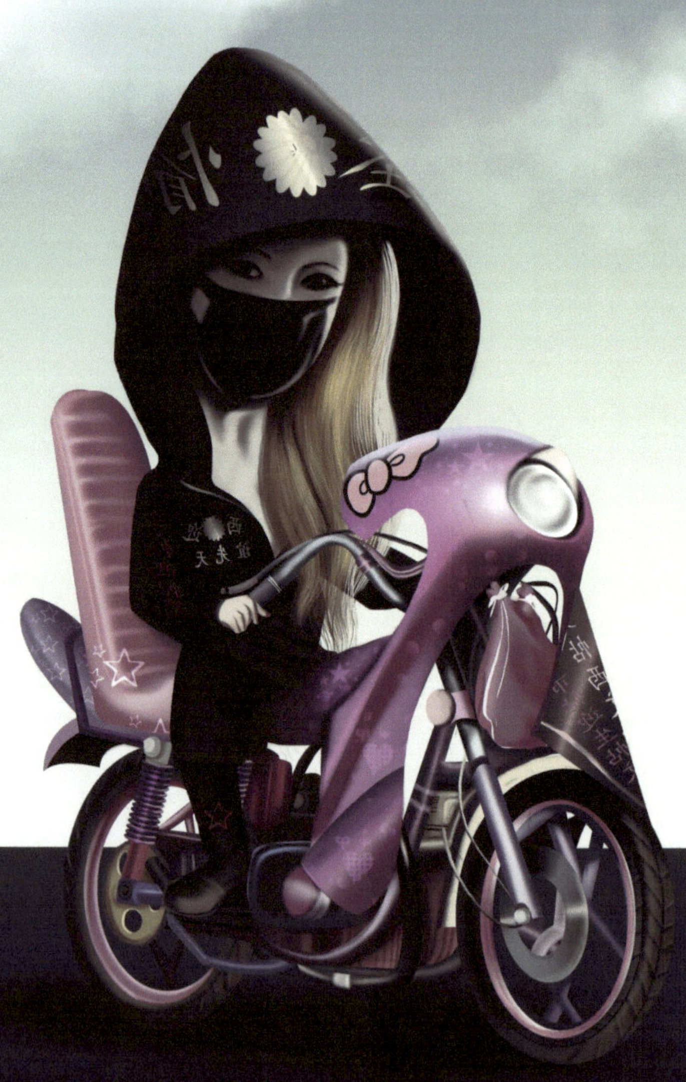